Spiritual Guidance from the Teachings of God's Anointed

To My Darling Grandson Cameron
To a Child of God.

Love From your Grandmother
Anita Cameron

Spiritual Guidance from the Teachings of God's Anointed

Anita Cameron

Copyright © 2009 by Anita Cameron.

ISBN: Hardcover 978-1-4363-9485-7
       Softcover 978-1-4363-9484-0

All rights reserved. No part of this book may be reproduced or transmitted in any form or by any means, electronic or mechanical, including photocopying, recording, or by any information storage and retrieval system, without permission in writing from the copyright owner.

This book was printed in the United States of America.

To order additional copies of this book, contact:
Xlibris Corporation
1-888-795-4274
www.Xlibris.com
Orders@Xlibris.com
56144

Acknowledgement

Pastor John Cherry Sr., Bishop Robert C. Blake Sr., Bishop Gilbert Earl Patterson

Dr. Creflo Dollar, Dr. Charles Stanley, Dr. Joseph Ripley,

Bishop Ellis 3rd, Detroit, Mi, Dr. Timothy Mitchell, Dr. Hillard

Dr. David Jeremiah, Pastor Duane Vanderklok, Pastor Vernon King,

Rev. Bill Winston, Doug Bachelor, Pastor Anthony Hines, Pastor Noel Jones,

Pastor Randy Morris, Pastor John Hagee,

and quotes by Grant Jeffrey of Bible Prophecy.

Matthew 10: 32
Whosoever therefore confess me before men, him will I confess also before my Father which is in heaven.

Matthew 10: 33
But whosoever shall deny me before men, him will I also deny before my Father which is in heaven.

Table of Contents

1. Maximizing Jesus our Almighty GOD 13
2. The Christ of Christmas 16
3. You are God's Masterpiece 20
4. What it means to walk in the Spirit Part # 1 23
5. What it means to walk in the Spirit Part # 2 25
6. God laid a plan out for all of us 28
7. Controlling the Tongue 32
8. Beware of the Devil (Satan) 34
9. Faith 36
10. Holy Ghost 40
11. The Landmine in the path of the believer 50
12. A Fervent Prayer 54
13. Amazing Grace 57
14. The practice of prayer in faith 59
15. God Has Us Sealed 61

Bible Study # 1
From the Teachings of
Pastor John Cherry, *Temper Hill, Maryland*

Maximizing the Birth of Jesus

Maximizing Jesus our Almighty God.
Maximizing Jesus the everlasting Father.

He gave us the power to act.
The right to act,
The will to act,
The responsibility to act,
When our will is to do His will, we cannot fail.

Jesus knew us before we were born. Our souls were in heaven before we came into this earth, therefore, while we were in our mother's womb. Jesus:

a. He weaved a body around our spirit.
b. He appointed parents unto us.
c. He gave us a time (A time to be born).
d. He gave us a gender (Male or Female).
e. He appointed us a race.
f. He appointed us times (span of time for each season of our life).
g. He appointed us a dwelling place (both naturally & spiritually).
h. He appointed us a day (determine whether we be with Him).
i. He determines your boundaries (Physically & spiritually).
   (He will never give you more than what you can bear).

Psalm 139: 1-6

1. *O Lord, you have searched me. And know me.*
2. *Thou knows my down sitting and mine uprising, thou understand my thought afar off.*
3. *Thou compassed my path and my lying down, and art acquainted with all my ways.*

4. *For there is not a word in my tongue, but, lo, O Lord, thou knows it altogether.*
5. *You have beset me behind and before and laid your hand upon me.*
6. *Such knowledge is too wonderful for me; it is high, I cannot attain unto it.*

Psalm 139: 13-16

13. *For thou have possessed my reins. You have covered me in my mother's womb.*
14. *I will praise you; marvelous are your works; and that my soul knows right well.*
15. *My substance was not hid from you, when I was made in secret, and curiously wrought in the lowest parts of the earth.*
16. *Your eyes did see my substance, yet being imperfect; and in thy book all my members were written, which in continuance were fashioned, when yet there was none of them.*

Psalm 139: 17
How precious also are thy thoughts unto me,. O God! How great is the sum of them.

Jesus Is Our Refuge

He said that perilous times would be in our life.
When we dwell in Him in perilous time

A. We dwell in a God with out evil.
B. We dwell in a God that gives power to the weak.
   What you are going through, God already knew.
C. We dwell in a God that renews our strength.

Read Isaiah 40:21-25, 26-31.

God does not want us to flop. He wants you to have wings of an Eagle.

Jesus is our Refuge in times yet to come.
Jesus is in our tomorrow.

1 Cor. 10:13
There have no temptation taken you but such as is common to man. But God is faithful, who will not suffer you to be tempted above that you are able; but will with the temptation also make a way to escape, that you may be able to bear it.

Read *Psalm 27: 1-4*
When I dwell in Him during perilous times,

A. He will hide me.
B. He will set me on a rock.
C. He will lift up my head above my enemy.
D. If others forsake me, the love of God will take me up.

Bible Study # 2
From: The teachings of
Dr. Charles Stanley, Atlanta, Georgia

The Christ of Christmas

Christmas is about Jesus
Who is Jesus?

Read, John 1: 1-4

In the beginning the word already existed. (The word being Jesus). He was with God, and He was God. He was in the beginning with God. He created everything there is. Nothing exists that He didn't make. Life itself was in Him, and this life gives light to everyone. The light shines through the darkness, and the darkness can never extinguish it.

He did not start at creation
He was there before creation
He was conceived by the Holy Ghost.

Luke 1: 35
And the angel answered and said unto her (Mary), the Holy Ghost shall come upon thee, and the power of the Highest shall overshadow thee; therefore also that Holy thing which be born of thee shall be call the Son of God.

He was born from a virgin

Luke 1: 26
And in the sixth month the angel Gabriel was sent from God unto a city of Galilee, named Nazareth.

Luke 1: 27
To a virgin espoused to a man whose name was Joseph, of the house of David; and the virgin's name was Mary.

Jesus is the eternal Son of God who had no beginning.

He is God
Remember, there's God the Father, God the Son and God the Holy Spirit.

When Jesus was asked, are you the Son of God? Jesus answered yes.

Luke 22: 70
Then said they all, art thou then the Son of God? And He said unto them, you say that I am

Jesus said "If you see me, you have seen the Father"

John 17: 9
Jesus said, "I pray for them, I pray not for the world but for them which you have given me; for they are yours."

John 17: 10
And all mine are yours and yours are mine; and I am glorified in them.

John 17: 11
And now I am no more in the world, but these are in the world and I come to you Holy Father, keep through your own name those whom you have given me that they may be one, as we are.

Jesus said "The Father loved me before the foundation of the world".

John 17: 20
Neither pray I for these alone, but for them also which shall believe in me through their word;

John 17: 21
That they all may be one; as thou, Father, are in me, and I in thee, that they also may be one in us, that the world may believe that you have sent me.

John 17: 22
And the glory which you gave me I have given them; that they may be one, even as we are one:

John 17: 23
I in them, and you in me, that they may be made perfect in one; and that the world may know that you have sent me, and have loved them, as you have loved me.

John 17: 26
Father, I will that they also whom you have given me, be with me where I am; they may behold my glory, which you have given me: For you loved me before the foundation of the world.

Jesus said "I always please the Father".

God is perfectly Holy so is Jesus.

Jesus said "No one comes to the Father except through me".

John 14: 6
Jesus said, "I am the way, the truth, and the life. No one can come to the father except through me.

John 14: 7
If you had known who I am, then you would have known who my father is. From now on you know Him and have seen Him.

If you give your thrust in me I will give you eternal life.
Ask and it shall be given, seek and you shall find, knock and the door shall be open.

Jesus came to redeem mankind. He came to be a ransom for us to save us from our sins.

It is all about Jesus who came to save us.

It is all about Jesus who died for us.

It is all about Jesus who took away our sins.

John 6: 38
Jesus said, "For I came down from heaven, not to do mine own will, but the will of Him that sent me.

John 6: 39
And this is the Father's will which has sent me that all which He has given me I should lose nothing, but should raise it up again at the last day.

John 6: 40
And this is the will of Him that sent me, that everyone which see the Son, and believe on Him, may have everlasting life: and I will raise Him up at the last day.

May the Lord add a blessing to His Holy Word.

Bible Study # 3
From the teachings of
Dr. Charles Stanley

You Are God's Masterpiece

Live an extraordinary Life

What does God see when He looks at us?

We see ourselves as being unfinished.

When God see us, He sees us as what we are and what we can be.

He sees us as we are and what we will become.

Read, Ephesians 2: 1-10

Workmanship—Thing of notable excellence (something above average)

The
Created work of God

A. Is that we can live out our lives in His purpose and plan.
B. God has predetermined that we are going to transform in the likeness of His Son.

Genesis 1:26
And God said, Let us make man in our image, after our likeness: and let them have dominion over the fish of the sea, and over the fowl of the air, and over everything that creep upon the earth.

He created us in His own image.

God's Plan for us

Jeremiah 29:11
For I know the thoughts that I think toward you, said the Lord, thoughts of peace, and not evil, to give you an expected end.

Ephesians 1:4
According as He has chosen us in Him before the foundation of the world, that we should be holy and without blame before Him in love.

Romans 8:29
For whom He knew before, He also did predestine to be conformed to the image of His Son, and that He might be the first born among many brethren.

Making us a Masterpiece

What is the process that God does to make it true?

1. We experience the new birth (born again).
2. We walk in the newness of life (Christ living inside of us).
3. Have a new family.

Romans 8: 16, 17
The Spirit itself bare witness with our spirit that we are the children of God.

And if children, the heirs; heirs of God, and joint—heirs with Christ. If so be that we suffer with Him, that we may be also glorified together.

4. A joint—heir with Jesus Christ

2nd Peter 1: 2
May God bless you with His special favor and wonderful peace as you come to know Jesus, our God and Lord, better and better.

2nd Peter 1: 3
As we know Jesus better, His divine power gives us everything we need for living a godly life. He has called us to receive His own glory and goodness!

> *2nd Peter 1: 4*
> *And by that same mighty power, He has given us all of His rich and wonderful promises. He has promised that you will escape the decadence all around you caused by evil desires and that you will share in His divine nature.*

We posses the Divine Nature of God

5. Has the awesome promise of His resources.
6. Have new Authority.

Read, 2 Peter 1: 5-8

> *Ephesians 2: 6*
> *God see us in Jesus, we are seated with God on His throne in Christ Jesus.*

Read, Act 1: 8

> *Jesus said, "When the Holy Spirit has come upon you, you will receive power and will tell people about me everywhere in Jerusalem, thoughout Judea, in Samaria and to the ends of the earth."*

7. Has power. *The Holy Spirit inside of us.*

    We have to accept who we are, and what we are in the eyes of God.

    The Spirit of God will enable you to do whatever God has for you.

8. Have a new Security.

    The Lord said "I will never leave you or forsake you".

9. Have a new purpose.

    Read Ephesians 1: 1, 2

10. Have a new destiny.

    Divine Nature cannot go the hell. As a believer, your destiny is set.

Bible Study # 4
From the teachings
of Dr. Creflo Dollar

What It Means To Walk In the Spirit (part 1)

Everything started with the Word (Christ Jesus).
Everything is hanging on His Word.
The world was created with His Word.

Ephesians 1: 3
Blessed be the God and Father of our Lord Jesus Christ, who has blessed us with all Spiritual blessings in heavenly places in Christ.

Therefore it is important that we read our Bible.
It must change our thinking.

You are not spiritual if you don't think and be in agreement with the Word of God.

The flesh is how we think and that contradicts the Word.

The Word says, "You are healed."
The flesh says, "You are sick."

If we walk by Faith and not by sight, we know that with His stripes I am healed.

God says it. You can.

When you walk in the Spirit, Satan has no control over you.

When you walk in the Spirit:

1. You know the promise of God.
2. He speaks to you.
3. Nothing can harm you.
4. He has power over you.
5. You have no fear.

Stay in the spirit

The Bible says we come from Royalty.
Stay in the Spirit and God will lift you up.
If you change your thinking today, your life will change forever.
Something's I won't do because I come from Royalty.
Everything that is, is hanging on the Word.

The enemy Satan the Devil

The enemy (Devil) wants you to believe that the Word is not true.
He wants you to disagree to what God wants you to do. He wants you to get out of the agreement with God.
Satan has no authority over your life when you walk in the Spirit.
The most power of the Devil (Satan) is suggestion.

Therefore, when you get out of your agreement with God, the Devil can control you.

But, if you stay in agreement with God, the Devil can't touch you.

Your mind, how you think will determine your destiny.

Your actions will have to line up with your thinking.

Bible Study # 5
From the teaching
of Dr. Creflo Dollar

What It Means To Walk in the Spirit (part 2)

Life on this planet is constantly trying to change our thinking.

It's trying to change your thinking of God, through the Media, television, music and people.

If you are thinking contrary to what God's Word, then you are thinking in the flesh, and it's all wrong.

Romans 12:1-2
1. I beseech you therefore, brethren, by the mercies of God, that you present your bodies a living sacrifice, holy, acceptable unto God, which is your reasonable service.
2. And be not conformed to this world: but be ye transformed by the renewing of your mind, that ye may prove what is good and acceptable, and the perfect will of God.

You come from Royalty,

Certain things I don't do, because my Royalty won't let me do those things.
If you think you will always be average all your life, and if that's how you think you will stay that way.
You cannot have strong thoughts of the world.

1. You can't just go to bed with anybody.
2. As a parent or guardian, you have to train your children in the Spirit.

3. Be in control of your child, keep-up on what they are doing.
4. Be honorable, your children will respect you.
5. Keep your mind set. Stop letting the norm and value of this society come into your children.

The Spirit Gives Life

I am blessed now already.
Tomorrow I am blessed already.
As long as you continue to talk this way, believe this way and think this way, you are *walking in the Spirit*.
Today I am blessed. Always I am blessed.
Regardless of what is in front of me, or what it looks like, my thinking must be as the Word. What the Bible says.
I must walk in the Spirit to get everything I want and need.
All blessing are in the Spirit.
To get evidence of your salvation start today.

John 6:63
Jesus said, "It is the Spirit that quickened. The flesh profits nothing; the words that I speak unto you, they are Spirit and they are life."

Walking and thinking that way profits you.

Walking in the flesh is no profit:

1. Telling people off.
2. Cursing people out.
3. Ego
4. Vanity

Slothfulness

Slothfulness is a gross violation of God.

Ephesians 4:1
Apostle Paul said, "I therefore the prisoner of the Lord, beseech you that he walk worthy of the vocation wherewith ye are called."

A slothful person:

1. Is going to have problems with relationships.
2. On the job problems.
3. Financial problems.
4. Going to feel pressure.

Do your best where you are.

God always honors us for doing the best we can.

Bible Study # 6
From the teachings of
Pastor John Cherry

God Laid A Plan Out For All Of Us

He made a plan for you.
He made a plan for me.

According to the plan that God laid down for you and I, were Justified by Faith.

Romans 5:1
Since we have been made right in God's sight by faith, we have peace with God because of what Jesus Christ our Lord has done for us.

Romans 5:2
Because of our faith, Christ has brought us into this place of highest privilege where we now stand, and we confidently and joyfully look forward to sharing God's glory.

Romans 5:3
We can rejoice too, when we run into problems and trials, for we know that they are good for us–they help us learn to endure.

Romans 5:10
For since we were restored to friendship with God by the death of His Son while we were still His enemies, we will certainly be delivered from eternal punishment by His life.

He did it by His Grace.

Ephesians 2:1
Once you were dead, doomed forever because of your many sins.

Ephesians 2:2
You use to live just like the rest of the world, full of sin, obeying Satan.

Ephesians 2:3
All of us use to live that way, following the passions and desires or our evil nature: We were born with an evil nature, and we were under God's anger just like everyone else.

Ephesians 2:4-5
But God is so rich in mercy, and He loves us so much, that while we were dead because of our sins, He gave us life when He raised Christ from the dead. (It is only by God's special favor that you have been saved.

After He *Justified* us He gave us *Grace* in His power *through the*

Holy Ghost.

Read, Ephesians 2: 6-10

After He *Justified* us, gave us *Grace*, He *Saved* us.

Read, Ephesians 2: 11-15

Without Jesus there is *no Peace.*

Jesus came because we couldn't live by the standard of the law.

a. We all sin.
b. We live by the flesh.
c. We didn't believe that Jesus died to save us, so that we *could* have *everlasting life.*
d. With all of this we had no peace. Know matter how much money we have.

But With Jesus

We can lay down all our Burdens.

a. We can lay down mistakes.
b. We can lay down guilt.
c. We can lay down anxiety.
d. We can lay down depression.

And that can stop all of us from thinking highly of ourselves instead of praising God.

Read, Ephesians 2: 16-18

You are all right with God as long as you are with Jesus.
Through Jesus we have peace with God.
Through Jesus we have peace with ourselves.
Through Jesus It was already done.
Having a homonymous relationship with ourselves.

Read Philippians 4: 7-9

He gave us instructions in His Word (Bible)

He *Instructed* us to:

a. Rejoice in the Lord.
b. Be anxious for nothing

Jesus said, "Come unto me all ye that labor and I will give you rest."

c. Have communication with the Lord through Prayer.
d. To think correctly.

Read Philippians 4: 8

e. He told us what to do to have peace of mind.

Read Philippians 4: 9

f. He said have no anxiety.

Anxiety is the devil's weapon to kill you.

1. Realize there are some things you cannot change.

    A. You can't change the rain.
    B. You can't make traffic move faster.
    C. You can't change people to be the way you want them to be.

But you can make the sun shine in you, whereas you won't worry about a thing because the Lord is there for you to give all things to Him.

Put all things in His hand. Before you do anything, pray on it. We have peace through God with Jesus Christ.

Read, Ephesians 4: 13

Therefore we will be:

1. Honest.
2. Full of the Holy Ghost.
3. Full of peace.

Peace with our brother.

A. If we build our Character.
B. Establish your conduct.—Our conduct is established by living according to our faith, full with the Spirit.
C. You have to defend your commitment to Christ.

Please Read, *Ephesians 4: 21-32*

Bible Study # 7
Bible study by Anita Cameron

Controlling the Tongue

James Chapter 3: 2-18

(2). we all make mistakes, but those who control their tongues can also control themselves in every other way.
(3). We can make a large horse turn around and go wherever we want by means of a small bit in its mouth.
(4). and a tiny rudder makes a huge ship turn wherever the pilot wants it to go, even though the winds are strong.
(5). also, the tongue is a small thing, but what enormous damage it can do. A tiny spark can set a great forest on fire.
(6). and the tongue is a flame of fire. It is full of wickedness that can ruin your whole life. It can turn the entire course of your life into a blazing flame of destruction, for it is set on fire by hell itself.
(7). People can tame all kinds of animals and birds and reptiles and fish,
(8). But, no one can tame the tongue. It is uncontrollable evil, full of deadly poison.
(9). Sometimes it praises our Lord and Father, and sometimes it breaks out into curses against those who have been made in the image of God.
(10). and so blessing and cursing come pouring out of the same mouth surely this is not right.
(11). Does a spring of water bubble out with both fresh water and bitter water?
(12). Can you pick olives from a fig tree or figs from a grapevine? No and you can't draw fresh water from a salty pool.
(13). If you are wise and understand God's ways, live a life of steady goodness so that only good deeds with pour forth, And you don't brag about the good you do, then you will be truly wise.
(14). But if you are bitterly jealous and there is selfish ambition in your hearts, don't brag about being wise. That is the worst kind of lie.

(15). for jealousy and selfishness are not God's kind of wisdom. Such things are earthly, unspiritual, and motivated by the Devil.
(16). for wherever there is jealousy and selfish ambition, there you will find disorder and every kind of evil.
(17). But the wisdom that comes from heaven is first of all pure. It is also peace loving, gentle at all times, and willing to yield to others. It is full of mercy and good deeds. It shows no partiality and is always sincere.
(18). and those who are peacemakers will plant seed of peace and reap a harvest of goodness.

MAY THE LORD ADD A BLESSING TO HOLY WORD.

Bible Study # 8
From the teaching of Pastor Cherry
Input also by Anita Cameron

Beware of the Devil (Satan)

God lined it all in the Word (Bible).

Satan comes to *Kill,* *Steal* and *Destroy.*

We let Satan in our mind to destroy.

Please note that Satan (devil) will utilize us to interfere in other people's life.

Sometimes you will find yourself feeling joy in your heart, then

1. The devil tries to work on you first by putting things in your head that is negative and ungodly. If he can't get you to lose his or her joy that way, then
2. He will work on someone else to get to you, to take away your joy.

For example:

You are a person that feels insecure about things. The devil will work on you continuously. If you ignore him, he then will try to get someone else to destroy your joy.
Or
You might see someone very happy and joyful and Satan will work on you to destroy their joy.

For example:

Someone could feel very good about how they look. The devil will work on you by putting things in your head like "that person thinks he or she is better than you, look how they are looking at you. You don't have to take that." Instead of you having control over your feelings or desires, you fall right into the devil trap, and say or do something rude to that person, destroying their joy.

How many times have you gone to the store to buy something and the devil has already gotten into the person waiting on you, and he or she say something derogatory to you. The devil starts working on you by putting in your mind, "are you going to take that." Then before you know it you have lost control and the two of you are arguing, taking away your joy. Satan at that very moment is laughing and kicking up his heels at the both of you.

Rev Cherry said that the success is when you are able to control those feelings and desires.

Most of all, like the apostle Paul said in Philippians 3: 2 Watch out for those dogs, those wicked men and their evil deeds.

Ephesians 6: 12
For we are not fighting against people made of flesh and blood, but against the evil rulers and authorities of the unseen world, against those mighty powers of darkness who rule this world, and against wicked spirits in the heavenly realms (high places).

Ephesians 6: 13
Use every piece of God's armor to resist the enemy in the time of evil days, so that after the battle you will still be standing firm.

Ephesians 6: 16
In every battle you will need faith as your shield to stop the fiery arrows aimed at you by Satan.

Ephesians 6: 17
Put on salvation as your helmet, and take the sword of the Spirit, which is the word of God.

Ephesians 6:18
Pray at all times and on every occasion in the power of the Holy Spirit. Stay alert and be persistent in your prayers for all Christians everywhere.

Bible Study # 9
From the teaching of Bishop Robert C. Blake Sr.
New Orleans, La

Faith

Now faith is the substance of things hoped for, the evidence of things not seen.

Faith Acts
Faith See the Answer.
Faith Put Me Beyond.
Faith puts my Sickness into My Healing.
Having Faith I look beyond.

What makes a Miracle?

It is something I can't do, but, I know the One that can.

There are times you need to be alone. You don't need any interruptions. You must have an intimate moment with the Master.

Prayer is our communication with God.

There's a secret in praying alone to deal with you and to deal with knowing yourself.

Hebrew 11:3
Through faith we understand that the worlds were framed by the word of God, so that things which are seen were not made of things which do appear

Hebrew 11: 6
But without faith it is impossible to please God. For he that come to God must believe that He is, and that He is rewarder of them that diligently seek Him.

Matthew 14:22
Jesus went to pray into the mountain while the disciples went into the ship. And the ship went into the mist of the sea.

Matthew 14:25
And in the fourth watch of the night, Jesus went unto them walking on the sea.

Matthew 14:26
And when the disciples saw Him walking on the sea, they were troubled, saying it is a spirit and they cried out of fear.

Matthew 14:27
But straightway Jesus spoke unto them, saying be of good cheer, it is I; be not afraid.

Matthew 14:28
And Peter answered Him and said, Lord, If it be you, bid me to come unto you on the water.

Matthew 14:29
And Jesus said to Peter, come. And when Peter came down off the ship, He walked on the water, to go to Jesus.

Matthew 14:30
But when he saw the wind boisterous, he was afraid, and began to sink. He cried out to the Lord, save me.

Matthew 14:31
And immediately Jesus stretched forth His hand and caught him, and said unto him, O you of little faith, why did you doubt?

Whatever your problem is, you have the Father working on it.

Teachings of Dr. Creflo Dollar

What is Faith?

Faith is a must to our spiritual life.

Luke 1: 45
And blessed is she that believed: for there shall be a performance of those things which were told her from the Lord.

Faith commands blessing, anointing, and it is a must for a meaningful victorious life.

Faith is blessing—When I develop in faith, I receive blessings.

2nd Peter 1:5
And beside this, giving all diligence, add to your faith virtue, and to virtue, knowledge.

Faith is the base line or foundation that you add things too. Add to your faith.

Faith is the base line to
Need Healing
Deliverance
Prosperity

Faith is the Foundation.

Psalm 11:3
If the foundation be destroyed, what can the righteous do?

Satan wants to destroy your faith.

When you get the word of God, you don't have to see it, but you have confirmation that it's yours.

Highest Dimension of faith

Hebrew 11: 32
Well, how much more do I need to say? It would take too long to recount the stories of the faith of Gideon, Barak. Samson, Jephthah, David, Samuel and all the prophets. By Faith these people overthrew kingdom, ruled with justice and received what God had promised them. They shut the mouths of lions.

Hebrew 11:34
Quenched the violence of fire, escaped death by the edge of the sword. Their weakness was turned into strength. They became strong in battle and put whole armies to flight.

Hebrew 11: 35
Women received their loved ones back again from death. but others trusted God and were tortured preferring to die rather than turn from God and be free. They placed their hope in the resurrection to a better life.

Through Faith we attain promises,

And these promises are given to us by His word.

It takes faith to get any results in the kingdom of God.

Faith is the producer of every good report.

Bible Study # 10
From the teaching of:
Dr. Joseph Ripley
Bishop Gilbert E. Patterson
Bishop Ellis
Dr. Creflo Dollar
Dr. Charles Stanley

The Holy Ghost is the author of the Bible

Dr. Ripley states "the gift of the Holy Ghost is the promise to those who receive Christ.

The Holy Ghost Is

1. Our Comforter
2. Our Teacher
3. God's Agent
4. Our Counselor
5. He Reveals things to us
6. He Brings things to our memory
7. He Guides us
8. He Empowers us
9. He Anoints us

That's why when you are baptized you are baptized in the name of the Holy Ghost.

You are empowered by the Holy Ghost's Super Natural Strength.

John 14:16
Jesus said I will ask the Father, and He will give you another Comforter, who will never leave you.

John 14: 17
He is the Holy Spirit, who leads into all truth. The world at large cannot receive, because it isn't looking for Him and don't recognize Him. But you do, because He lives with you now and later will be in you.

John 14: 18
No, I will not abandon you as orphans. I will come to you.

John 14:26
The comforter, which is the Holy Spirit whom the Father will send in my name, He shall teach you all thing, and bring all Things to your membrane of whatsoever I have said to you.

Jesus was anointed by the Holy Ghost while He was on the earth.

Before Christ was sent down to earth The Holy Ghost was sent down to empower the prophets to give the word of God to the people.

Solomon was anointed with great strength, knowledge and wisdom.

Jesus didn't preach or heal unless the Holy Ghost was anointing Him.

The same anointing Jesus received comes on His people.

The Holy Ghost gives us
Power
And He Seals us

Gelatians 3:14
That the blessing of Abraham might come on the Gentiles Through Jesus Christ that we might receive the promise of The Holy Spirit through faith.

When I live according to my faith I receive Spiritual blessings.

It is a promise that the Holy Ghost will reside in me, and I will receive the power of the Holy Ghost.

I am empowered by the Holy Spirit working inside of me.

And we all will have power to heal.

Empowered with the Holy Ghost.

Bishop Gilbert E Patterson said,

"The Holy Ghost will guide you. You can't make it by yourself; you have to have a guide.

If you don't have the Holy Ghost, you don't have the receiver.

The Holy Ghost is the intercessor.

When you want God to fill you with the Holy Ghost, the Holy Ghost wants to hear what you say.

When the Holy Ghost hears what you say,
He says it in tongues.

People that are taught by man to speak in tongues are not speaking in tongues through the Holy Ghost.

Ex:

Some people after being saved want to impress others into thinking they have received the Holy Ghost through speaking in unknown tongues. They will have someone teach them what to say or how to say certain words."

Don't ever try to lie to the Holy Ghost.

When Jesus went back up to Heaven, the Holy Ghost came down.

1st John 5: 7
For there are three that bear record in heaven, the Father, the word Christ
and the Holy Ghost
And these three are one.

Bishop Ellis the third said,

"Love through the Fruit of the Spirit."

Romans 5:5
And hope make not ashamed because the love of God is shed abroad in our hearts by the Holy Ghost which is given unto us.

"The day you got born again the Holy Ghost released that package—the love package.

The Holy Ghost is the one responsible for pouring out the love package to the child of God.

The Holy Ghost injects the love of God.

God is love—the Holy Ghost came to deliver love to us, and deliver God in you.

You are now posses with love and you're possessed with God.

God's in there, and that's why when the devil (Satan) shows up he can't survive.

The Holy Spirit injects the love of God in our hearts."

Matthew 22:37
Jesus said, "You must love the Lord your God with all your heart, all your soul, and your entire mind.

Matthew 22:38
This is the first and greatest commandment.

"This type of love is only given by the injection, by the Holy Ghost.

Human love will or might fail, because things didn't go the way you wanted them too.

But, when you love that person that love God more than they love you, then you have the right person to humanly love.

Human type of love is selfish.

The Holy Ghost injects a Super Natural Love."

Dr. Creflo Dollar said,

"The coming of the Holy Ghost is going to be to your advantage, Jesus said "I go away so that the comforter can come".

The Holy Ghost is the key to our success in life.
There is a path to every objective in life.

A path that leads to life.

A path that leads to death.

A path that leads to education.

A path that leads to doing nothing for yourself.

We will no longer leave the Holy Ghost out of anything.

The Holy Ghost has been sent with an assignment.

The Holy Ghost is trying to show you something.

The key to supernatural success is when you spend time with the Holy Ghost, our unseen partner.

Jesus said when you see me you see the Father and when you see the Holy Ghost you see me.

The Holy Ghost wants to show you something. If he shows you something it will be your help and comfort."

Bishop Gilbert Earl Patterson said,

"A new look at the Holy Ghost."

Love is the most excellent way.

*1 Corinthians **12:30***
Have all the gifts of healing? Do all speak with tongues? do all interpret? Are you all prophets?

Everybody's not a prophet.

Mark 16:17
And these signs shall follow them that believe; in my name shall they cast out devils, they shall speak with new tongues.

Spiritual Gifting

1 Corinthians 12: 28
First are apostles.
Second are prophets.
Third are teachers.
Those who do miracles.
Those who have the gift of healing.
Those who can help others.
Those who get others to work together.
And those who speak in unknown tongues.

1 Corinthians 12:29
Is everyone an apostle? of course not. Is everyone a prophet? No. Are all teachers? Does everyone have the power to do miracles? Does everyone have the gift of healing? Of course not. Does God give all of us the ability to speak in unknown languages? No. And in any event you should desire the most helpful gifts, Love is the Greatest.

Love is Greatest

*1 Corinthians **12:31***
And in any event you should desire the most helpful gifts. Love is the greatest. First however, let me tell you about something else that is better that any of them.

1 Corinthians 13:1
If I could speak in any language in heaven or on earth, but didn't love others, I would only be making meaningless noise like a loud gong or a clanging cymbal.

1 Corinthians 13:2
If I had the gift of prophecy, and if I knew all the mysteries of the future and knew everything about everything, but didn't love others what good would I be? And If I had the gift of faith so that I could speak to a mountain and make it move without love I would be no good to anybody.

If I don't have love it profits me nothing.

Prophecy is a better gift than speaking in tongues

1 Corinthians 14:2
For if your gift is the ability to speak in tongues, you will be talking to God but not to people, since they won't be able to understand you. You will be speaking by the power of the Spirit, but it will all be mysterious.

1 Corinthians 14: 3
But one who prophesies is helping other grow in the Lord encouraging and comforting them.

1 Corinthians 14: 4
A person who speaks in tongues is strengthened personally in the Lord, but one who speaks a word of prophecy strengthens the entire church.

The Holy Ghost can give us the ability to speak in another language we didn't go to school for.

Unknown Tongues

There is a language in heaven, you can't learn it in school, but when the Holy Ghost comes in the room you will know.
Because the Holy Ghost is there to give the interpretation Hallelujah.

I found out many people were taught how to speak in tongues.

You cannot learn how to speak in tongues. It must come from the power of the Holy Ghost, If you are relating to God.

People cannot take you into a room and teach you how to talk in unknown tongues, because it doesn't come from man it comes from God and the Holy Ghost.

Jesus Promises Living Water

John 7:37
On the last day, the climax of the festival, Jesus stood and shouted to the crowds, If you are thirsty come to me!

John 7: 38
If you believe in me, come and drink! For the Scriptures declare that rivers of living water will flow out from within.

John 7:39
(When He said "living water", He was speaking of the Spirit, who would be given to everyone believing in Him. But the Spirit had not yet been given because Jesus had not yet entered into His glory).

Matthew 10:18
Jesus said, "And you must stand trial before governors and kings because you are my followers. This will be your opportunity to tell them about me. Yes, to witness to the world".

Matthew 10:19
When you are arrested, don't worry about what to say in your defense, because you will be given the right words at the right time.

Matthew 10:20
For it won't be you doing the talking, it will be the Spirit of your Father speaking through you.

Matthew 12:30
Jesus said "He that is not with me is against me; and he that gathered not with me scattered abroad.

Matthew 10:31
Every sin or blasphemy can be forgiven, except blasphemy against the Holy Spirit, which can never be forgiven.

Matthew 10:32
Anyone who blasphemes against me, the Son of Man can be forgiven, but blasphemy against the Holy Spirit will never be forgiven, either in this world or in the world to come.

Acts 1:8
Jesus said "But when the Holy Spirit has come upon you, you will receive power and will tell people about me everywhere, in Jerusalem, throughout Judea, in Sumaria, and to the ends of the earth.

Acts 1:5
Jesus said, "John baptized with water, but in just a few days you will be baptized with the Holy Spirit.

Living in the Power of the Holy Spirit

Gifts of the Spirit

Dr. Charles Stanley said,

1st Peter 4: 10
God has given gifts to each of you from His great variety of spiritual gifts. Manage them well so that God's generosity can flow through you.

1st Peter 4:11
Are you called to be a speaker? Then speak as though God Himself were speaking through you. Are you called to help others? Do it with all the strength and energy that God supplies. Then God will be given glory in everything through Jesus Christ. All glory and power belong to Him forever and ever Amen.

We are given gifts, and one of these gifts is in you. It is the motivating gift within you.

The Holy Spirit will motivate our gifts

God's gift to you is His purpose for you because He knows what He wants you to accomplish in your life. The knowledge of it affects our lives and our relationship with others.

The gift of Service

Service in the *Spirit*	Service in the *Flesh*
1. Alert to others need	1. Unconscious of needs
2. Hospitable	2. Loner
3. Generous	3. Stingy
4. Joyful	4. Self-pity
5. Flexibility	5. Inflexible
6. Available	6. Self-centered
7. Endurance	7. No energy

The source of your strength is God. Whatever you need, God gives you the pure strength of Him.

Whatever God gives you to do, He gives you His strength.

Remember, Philippians 4:13
I can do all things through Christ who strengthens me.

Bible Study # 11
From the teachings of
Dr. Charles Stanley

The Land Mine in the Path of the Believer

Satan lays his land mine that will utterly destroy us.

a. Jealousy
b. Pride
c. Insecurity
d. Anger

Insecurity

A feeling of being inadequate of doing or facing things in life.

a. Not accepted
b. Disapproved of
c. Inner turmoil

Why do people feel insecure?

1. Sometimes—unpredictable childhood environment.
2. Experience Tragedy.
    a. A mother dies
    b. Failures in life—Financial

Divorce

3. Understanding skills and talents with encouragement.

4. Living under unrealistic rules and regulations.
    a. Sometimes are substitutes of what the parent should be doing.
    b. Totally out of reach of what a person should or can do.

5. A poor body image.
6. Growing up without positive feedback.
7. Unsecured beliefs.
    a. I can never accomplish this task.
    b. I can't do it.
    c. I am a failure.
    d. I am ugly.
    e. I am a loser.
    f. They are only being nice to me because they want something.

Whatever you tell yourself and the way you imagine yourself to be is the way you become.

Your imagination is the strongest thing in your life and what you image yourself to be is the way you become.

Effects of Insecurity

1. A difficult time establishing good and lasting relationships.

    All of us need strong Godly relationships with each other.

2. Being perceived as snobbish and prude.
3. Indecisiveness.
    a. Can't make decisions.
    b. Fearful—never being able to enjoy the life God has for you.

4. Afraid of Failure.
    a. Limit what God can do in your life.

5. Anger
    a. You want to condemn someone else.
    b. They want to pull somebody down.

6. Passed over for promotions and honors.
7. Problems meeting others and having relationships.

You can't compare yourself with others.

8. Believing that success is based on the approval of others.

    Success is following the will of God and accomplishing the things He wants you to.

9. You do your best to hide it.
    a. The proudest people are usually the most insecure.
    b. Loud mouth people.
    c. Boasting, and Bragging.

    When you trust Jesus Christ as your savior, there's peace, joy and you feel secure.

    A personal relationship with Jesus Christ can be had, by reading the Bible.

How You Over Come Being Insecure?

1. The love of God.
2. Acknowledge your feelings and identify the causes.
3. Make a decision to overcome it in Christ.
4. You have to realize that it is more than self-esteem.
    A. Am I the way I see myself or am I not.

    We cannot see how other people see us.

5. We ask "how does God see me?
6. Don't focus on negative feelings. Focus on the Holy Ghost in us.
7. Focus on the positive qualities in your life.

    Trust God for what is not as if it were until it becomes a reality.

8. Visualize.
    a. That you prepare and pre-plan your responses.

    You should get up saying; I am good, saved by Grace, and I am a child of the Living God.

9. Feel your mind with the present of God's word.

God will let you overcome.

10. Stop comparing yourself with other people.
11. Avoid the trap of blaming others. Accept the fact that's where you are.
12. Reward yourself when you do the right thing.
13. Overcome any doubts about the word of God.

There is nothing God cannot do to bring you out of insecurity, pride and jealousy.

Bible Study # 12
Teaching of
Dr. Creflo Dollar

A Fervent Prayer

Speaking God's language, how you pray.

To get the results you need, don't limit God's power from your life.

You have got to learn how to believe God, and stir up faith,
Stay in Faith.

Staying in Faith means,

1. We live by faith.
2. We are healed by faith.
3. It keeps our marriages together by faith.
4. Our needs and wants are met by faith.
5. No matter what comes we shall live by faith.

Stay in faith

You don't let the devil handle you.

John 14:13
Jesus said "You can ask anything in my name, and I will do it, because the work of the Son brings glory to the Father".

John 14:14
Jesus said "Yes ask anything in my name and I will do it.

If you ask Jesus He will do it.

Answering prayer is no man's idea, its God's idea.

Reasons for prayer not answered.

1. Wrong motives and methods.
2. Sometimes the way we pray.
   a. Praying for show.
   b. Praying loud to be noticed.
   c. Praying selfish prayers.

The Kingdom of God is concerned about others, not selfish prayers.

Romans 8:29
For God knew His people in advance, and He chose them to be like His Son. So that His Son will be the first born with many brothers and sisters.

When we pray we get results. We are destined to be just like Jesus. Jesus received everything he asked for. So can we.

Ephesians 6:18
Pray at all times and on every occasion in the power of the Holy Spirit. Stay alert and be persistent in your prayers for all Christians everywhere

There are all kinds of prayers.

1. Prayers that changes things.

   a. The prayer of agreement. Where two or more shall agree as one.
   b. The prayer of faith will change things by using the scriptures.
   c. Prayer of Petition.
   d. Prayer of binding and loosing to forbid something.
   e. The prayer of intercession—Praying for someone else.
   f. United prayer.

2. Prayer of Thanksgiving and Praise
   a. Spending time thanking God for everything and praising Him.

By doing so, you are producing a weapon that is attacking your enemy.

Always say the prayer of dedication and consecration.

Cast all your cares on the Lord.

1st Peter 5:7
Give all your worries and cares to God, for He cares about what happens to you.

You are not supposed to worry about anything. You are to give all your worries and cares to the Lord.

You are to say I am not supposed to be broke, busted or discussed. I am a child of the living God.

You have to do that before you pray. You have to get mess off of you.

When you pray you must have faith, and leave everything in God's hand.

Bible Study # 13
From the teaching of
Dr. Timothy Mitchell
Dr. Creflo Dollar

Amazing Grace

We are to praise and set apart the name of God.

Jehovah God

When you say revealing Himself, the eternal changeless one is revealing His ways to us.

He reveals Himself as:

JEHOVAH—JIREH—Provider
JEHOVAH—ROPHE—Healer
JEHOVAH—NISSI—Battle Fighter
JEHOVAH—SHALOM—Given of peace
JEHOVAH—TSIDKENU—Our righteousness
JEHOVAH—SHAMMAH—Ever present one
JEHOVAH—ROHI—Good Shepherd
JEHOVAH—M'KADDESH—Our Sanctifier

Eight compound names of God.

The Amazing Grace

1. Is when God opens doors, where there are no doors? It just seems impossible.

JEHOVAH—NISSI, JEHOVAH SHAMMAH.

2. When you are sick and told there's nothing they can do, and God heals you.

   JEHOVAH—JIREH, JEHOVAH—SHAMMAH, JEHOVAH—ROPHE.

3. When everything or everybody seems to be against you—God's amazing Grace brings you through. Whereas you though it was the end or final and fear set in.

   JEHOVAH—ROHI, JEHOVAH—TSIDKENU, JEHOVAH—NISSI, JEHOVAH—SHALOM.

   When you think everything is lost and gone, God's amazing Grace appears.

   JEHOVAH-SHALOM.

   Exodus 3:13
   Moses said unto God, behold, when I come unto the children of Israel, and shall say unto them, The God of your fathers has sent me unto you. And they shall say to me, what is His name? What shall I say unto them?

   Exodus 3: 14
   And God said unto Moses, I AM ThAT I AM. And He said, this is what you shall say unto the children of Israel, I AM has sent me unto you.

   Exodus 3: 15
   And God said moreover unto Moses. You shall say to the children of Israel, The Lord God of your fathers, The God of Abraham, The God of Issac, and the God of Jacob has sent me unto you: This is my name forever, and this my memorial unto all generations.

   That name allows Him to be whatever you need Him to be.

   JEHOVAH—The everlasting God, the healer, the one who didn't let me go crazy, who is merciful and great.

   The purpose of learning God's name is to have closeness to Him and getting a knowing of who He is.

Bible Study # 14
From the teaching of Bishop Ellis
of Detroit, Michigan

The Practice of Prayer In Faith

Faith is the ability to live in a limited world in an unlimited way.

If you apply faith to your prayer, folks cannot comprehend.

Walk by faith not by sight.

Faith says God can do what sight can't.

God can make a way out of no way.

All you have to do is sit and wait.

When you wait in faith it doesn't seem to be so long.

Sometimes you walk by faith with your eyes close, because it looks worst than what it is.

Faith can only please God.

Psalms 31: 1

In thee O Lord, do I put my thrust; let me never be ashamed: deliver me in your righteousness.

Praise the Lord for what He's done and what He's going to do.
He is able to make good on His promise.
God inhabits the praises of His people.

I've got to praise God for what He's done and for
what He's going to do.

Take every step by faith,
God gives to you in His time.
Stops letting the devil magnify things in your face.
Prayer goes both ways, God might have some stuff He wants you to
get out of you.

Hebrew 11:1
*Now faith is the substance of things hoped for, the evidence of things not
seen.*

Hebrew 11: 3
*Through faith we understand that the worlds were framed by the word of
God, so that things which are seen were not made of things which appear.*

Hebrew 11:6
*But without faith it is impossible to please Him. For he that come to God
must believe that He is, and that He is a rewarder of them that diligently
seeks Him.*

Bible Study # 15
From the teaching of
Bishop Ellis 3rd

God Has Us Sealed

Great is the mystery of Godliness.

God reserves some things for Himself.

God gives you a sneak view of what He has for you.

Every now and then, God rolls back the curtain of heaven to give you a sneak peak.

Every once in awhile God will put something in you and show you something.

God drops things in our spirit.

He allows us to get a glimpse of our inheritance.

It's always better to wait on the Lord.

He may not come when we want Him to, but He always comes on time.

Look at what you have.

Greater things are what God has for you.

The things that are seen, is temporary life. But, the unseen is eternal life.

He gives us some spiritual things now.

When God changed me in a twinkling of eye, I received my inheritance.

We are covered and sealed until He comes.

JESUS MAKES ThE DIFFERENCE

God has empowered me with anything I do.

If I don't utilize the gifts that God gives to me, He will take it away
and give it to someone else.
He can take it back anytime He wants to.
We are to look to Jesus for our power and deliverance.

Table of Contents

1. Controlling your thinking 65
2. JESUS Is the Word 67
3. Iniquities 79
4. Unexpected Challenges 83
5. Trusting God 87
6. The Will of God 89
7. Facing the Unknown 93
8. Walking in Authority 97
9. Master Your Emotions 100
10. Anti-Christ 103
11. Love in its highest form 106
12. The Heavenly City 110
13. How to get your prayers answered 114
14. Redeemed from Death 116
15. Surrounded by Enemies 120

Bible Study # 16
From the teachings of
Bishop Robert C. Blake

Controlling your thinking

Taking the youth back to the altar.

Always know that your destiny lives in you.

Whatever you need is in you.

You have to develop yourself, and keep focus.

Know that something in you can raise you up.

The Lord raises you up.

God gave you to the world to be a blessing.

You are different and God made you that way.

Whenever you try being someone else, you spend all that time not being you.

Develop yourself.

You can do more for yourself than anyone in the world can.

You have got to know who you are, and who's you are.

YOU ARE A CHILD OF GOD.

Therefore:

    a. Love you.
    b. Take time with you.
    c. Discipline you.
    d. Spend time to pray and read the Word (Bible).
    e. Time to rise up now and do what you've never done before.
    f. Make an assessment for yourself.
    g. All imagination isn't bad, so don't give up your imagination.
    h. You have to be against that which is against God.

We must understand who we are.
We are going to be rich.
We are born to be rich

Our weapons are mighty through God.
Sometimes I get knocked down, but I get right up.

Ephesians 6:16
In every battle you need faith as your shield to stop the fiery arrows aimed at you by Satan.

Ephesians 6:17
Put on salvation as your helmet, and take the sword of the Spirit, which is the word of God.

Ephesians 6: 18
Pray at all times and on every occasion in the power of the Holy Spirit. Stay alert and be persistent in your prayers for all Christians everywhere.

Bible Study # 17
From the teaching of Bishop Robert C. Blake,
Bishop Gilbert Earl Patterson,
Dr. Creflo Dollar
Input also by Anita Cameron

Jesus is the Word

John 1: 1
In the beginning the Word already existed, He was with God and He was God.

John 1: 2
He was in the beginning with God.

John 1: 3
He created everything there is. Nothing exists that He didn't make.

John 1: 4
Life itself was in Him, and the life gives light to everyone.

John 1: 5
The light shines through the darkness, and the darkness can never extinguish the light.

John 1: 10
But although the world was made by Him. The world didn't recognize Him when He came.

John 1: 14
So the Word became human and lived here on earth among us. He was full of unfailing love and faithfulness. And we have seen His glory of the only begotten Son of the Father.

The Birth of Christ

Bishop Robert C. Blake said,

"The birth of Christ is the Super Natural Birth that came to earth."

"God is a mystery, and He showed us how serious His love for us is."

Dr. Creflo Dollar said,

"If Jesus wasn't born we would have a horrible existence."

Romans 5: 21
So just as sin ruled over all people and brought them to death, now God's wonderful kindness rules instead, giving us right standing with God and resulting in eternal life through Jesus Christ our Lord.

Jesus's Super Natural Birth

*Luke **1:26***
God sent the angel Gabriel to Nazareth, a village in Galilee,

Luke 1: 27
to a virgin named Mary. She was engaged to be married to a man named Joseph, a descendant of King David.

Luke 1:28
Gabriel appeared to her and said, "Greeting s favored woman, the Lord is with you.

Luke 1:29
Confused and disturbed, Mary tried to think of what the angel meant.

Luke 1: 30
Gabriel said, "Don't be frightened Mary, for God has decided to bless you".

Luke 1: 31
You will become pregnant and have a son, and you are to name Him Jesus.

Luke 1: 32
He will be very great and will be called the Son of the Most High. And the Lord God will give Him the throne of His ancestor David.

Luke 1: 33
And He will reign over Israel forever, for His Kingdom will never end.

Luke 1: 34
Mary asked the angel, "But how can I have a baby? I am a virgin".

Luke 1:35
The angel replied, "The Holy Spirit will come upon you, and the power of the Most High God will overshadow you. So the baby born to you will be holy, and He will be called the Son of God.

Matthew 1: 18
Now this is how Jesus the Messiah was born. His mother, Mary was engaged to be married to Joseph. But while she was still a virgin, she became pregnant by the Holy Spirit,

Matthew 1: 19
Joseph, her fiancée, being a just man, decided to break the engagement off quietly, so as not to disgrace her publicly.

Matthew 1:20
As he considered this, he fell asleep, and an angel of the Lord appeared to Him in a dream. "Joseph son of David," The angel said, "do not be afraid to go ahead with your marriage to Mary. For the child within her has been conceived by the Holy Spirit.

Matthew 1: 21
And she will have a son, and you are to name Him Jesus, for He will save His people from their sins.

Matthew 1: 22
All of this happened to fulfill the Lord's message through His prophet.

Matthew 1; 23
*"Look! The virgin will conceive a child! She will give birth to a son, And He will be called Immanuel
Meaning God is with us.*

Luke 2:11
For unto you is born this day in the city of David a Savior, which is Christ the Lord.

Luke 2: 12
And this shall be a sign unto you; You shall find the baby wrapped in swaddling clothes, lying in a manger.

More than three Shepards came. They came with gifts.

Gold—To honor His Kingship.
Myrrh—Rub Him down with aloe when he died.
Frankincense—High Priest.

God came in the flesh, He came in sinful flesh, so that He could condemn sin in the flesh. And if you receive Him, you can live a victorious life through Him.

Jesus grew as a man.
Living He love me,
Dying He took my sins away.

One day He's coming back, and that will be a glorious day.

Read
Revelations: 12 it is about the Past, Present and Future.

Satan tried to abort and devour the child Jesus before He was born. But, the child was caught up unto God and to His throne. Satan can't kill Him.

John 1: 14
And the Word became human and lived here on earth among us. He was full of unfailing love and faithfulness. And we have seen His glory of the only begotten Son of the Father.

Jesus intercedes for us,

That's why He came down to earth so that He could take away our sins and bring us back into the presents of God. So that we can be saved by grace and have ever lasting life.

Before Christ came to earth, death was a final thing. When a person died they returned to dust. Except those that God found favor in.

But Jesus came and bared all our burdens and sins so that we could someday come into the present of our Father.

Jesus death had a purpose. He could have at anytime stopped what was happening to Him, but to save us He paid it all.

Jesus was falsely accused.

Matthew 26:59
The high priests, conspiring with the Jewish Council, tried to cook up charges against Jesus in order to sentence Him to death.

Matthew 26:60
But even though many stepped up making one false accusation after another, nothing was believable.

Mark 14:57
Then some stood up and gave the false testimony against Him.

Mark 14:60
Then the high priest stood up before them and asked Jesus, "Are you going to answer? What is this testimony that these men are bringing against you?"

Mark 14:61
But Jesus remained silent and gave no answer. Again the high priest asked Him, "Are you the Christ, the Son of the Blessed one?

Mark 14:62
Jesus said. "I am and you will see the Son of man sitting at the right hand of the Mighty one and coming on the clouds of heaven."

Mark 14:64
The high priest said, "You have heard the blasphemy. What do you think?" They all condemned Him as worthy of death.

Mark 14:65
Then some began to spit at Him; they blindfolded Him, struck Him with their fists, and said "Prophesy!" And the guard took Him and beat Him.

John 19:1
Then Pilate took Jesus and had Him whipped.

John 19:2
The soldiers twisted together a crown of thorns and put it on His head. They clothed Him in a purple robe.

John 19:3
And went up to Him again and again, saying, "hail, King of the Jews!" and they struck Him in the face.

Jesus suffered, but never gave up His purpose on this earth. Even though His apostles scattered when He was arrested, and Peter denied knowing Him.

Jesus's Crucifixion

Jesus revealed so much to people while He walked the earth.

1. He healed the sick.
2. He raised people from the dead.
3. He healed people that were demon possessed.
4. He taught people about the Kingdom of God.
5. On several occasions He fed thousands with a meal meant for one person.
6. He showed His glory on the mountain where Moses and Elias met Him and God spoke through a cloud saying, "This is my beloved Son listen to Him."

Yet He was alone in His suffering.

He could have at anytime stopped things from happening to Him, but He chose to stay and finish what He came down to achieve for us.

Jesus was crucified. While He was nailed to the cross people made fun of Him.

The Crucifixion Of Jesus

Matthew 27:31
After they had mocked Jesus, they took off the robe and put His own clothes on Him. Then they led Him away to crucify Him.

John 19:16
So the soldier took charge of Jesus, carrying His own cross, He went to the place of the skull.

Mark 15:21
A certain man from Cyrene, named Simon, the father of Alexander and Rufus, was passing by on His way in from the country and they forced Him to carry the cross.

Mark 15:22
They brought Jesus to the place called Golgotha (which means the place of the skull).

Mark 15:23
Then they offered Jesus wine mixed with myrrh and He refused it.

Mark 15:24
Ands they crucified Him, dividing up His clothing then cast lots to see what each would get.

Mark 15:25
It was the third hour when they crucified Him (9AM)

Mark 15:27
They crucified two robbers with Him, one on His right and one on His left.

Mark 15:29
Those who passed by hurled insults at Him, shaking their heads and saying. So! You who are going to destroy the temple and build it in three days.

Mark 15: 30
Come down from the cross and save yourself!

Mark 15:31
The leading priest and teacher of religious law also mocked Jesus, saying "He saved others, but, He can't save Himself."

Mark 15:33
At the 6th hour which is noon, darkness fell across the whole land until three o'clock.

Mark 15:35
Then at that time Jesus called out with a loud voice Eloi, Eloi, lema Sabachthani?" Which means, "My God, My God why have you forsaken me?

Mark 15:38
And the curtain in the temple was torn in two from top to bottom.

Luke 23:46
Then Jesus shouted, "Father I entrust my spirit into your hands!" And with those words He breathed His last.

Matthew 27: 51
At the moment the curtain of the temple was torn from the top to bottom, the earth shook and the rocks split.

Matthew 27: 52
The tombs broke open and the bodies of many holy people who had died were raised to life.

Matthew 27: 53
They came out of the tombs, and after Jesus' resurrection, they went into the holy city and appeared to many people.

Jesus Burial

John 15:12
This all happened on Friday, the day of preparation, the day before the Sabbath.

John 19: 38
Later, Joseph of Arimathea asked Pilate for the body of Jesus. But secretly because he feared the Jews, with Pilate's permission, he came and took the body away.

John 19: 39
He was accompanied by Nicodemus, the man who earlier had visited Jesus at night. Nicodemus brought a mixture of Myrrh and aloes, about seventy five pounds,

John 19:40
Taking Jesus body, the two of them wrapped it, with the spices, and in strips of linen. This was in accordance with Jewish burial customs.

John 19: 41
At the place where Jesus was crucified, there was a garden, and in the garden a new tomb, in which no one had ever been laid.

Jesus was laid in that tomb.

The Resurrection Of Jesus

Luke 24: 1
But very early on Sunday morning the women came to the tomb, taking the spices they had prepared.

Luke 24: 2
They found that the stone covering the entrance had been rolled aside.

Luke 24: 3
So they went in, but they couldn't find the body of the Lord Jesus.

Luke 24: 4
They were puzzled trying to think what could have happened to His body. Suddenly, two men appeared to them, clothed in dazzling robes.

Luke 24: 5
The woman were terrified and bowed low before them. Then the men asked. "Why are you looking in a tomb for someone who is alive?

Luke 24: 6
He isn't here! He has risen from the dead! Don't you remember what He told you back in Galilee.

Luke 24: 7
That the Son of man must be betrayed into the hands of sinful men and be crucified, and that He would rise again the third day?"

Jesus Appears To His Disciples

*John **20: 17***
Jesus said to Mary Magdalene, when she saw Him at the garden, "Don't touch me. For I have not yet ascended to the Father. But go find my brothers and tell them that I am ascending to my Father and your Father, my God and your God."

John 20: 19
That evening on the first day of the week, the disciples were meeting behind locked doors because they were afraid of the Jewish leaders. Suddenly, Jesus was standing there among them! "Peace be with you." He said

Luke 24:25
Then Jesus said to them "You are such foolish people! You find it so hard to believe all that the prophets wrote in the Scriptures.

Luke 24: 26
Wasn't it clearly predicted by the prophets that the Messiah would have to suffer all these things before entering His time of glory?"

Luke 24: 27
Then Jesus quoted passages from the writings of Moses and all the prophets, explaining what all the Scriptures said about Himself.

John 20: 20
As He spoke, He held out His hands for them to see and He showed them His side. They were filled with joy when they saw their Lord!

John 20: 21
He spoke to them again and said, "Peace be with you. As the Father has sent me, so I send you.

John 20: 22
Then He breathed on them and said to them, "Receive the Holy Spirit".

John 20: 23
If you forgive anyone's sins, they are forgiven. If you refuse to forgive them, they are unforgiving.

1st Corinthians 4: 6
After that Jesus was seen of above 500 brethren at once.

Luke 24: 50
Then Jesus led them to Bethany and lifting His hands to heaven, He blessed them.

Luke 24: 51
While He was blessing them, He left them and was taken up to heaven.

Luke 24: 52
They worshipped Him and then returned to Jerusalem filled with great joy.

Luke 24: 53
And they spent all of their time in the Temple praising God.

1st Corinthians 15: 21
For since by man came death, by man came also the resurrection of the dead.

1st Corinthians 15: 22
For as in Adam all die, even so in Christ shall all be made alive.

Therefore when Adam sinned, death was to all. But, when Jesus was crucified and resurrected He took away all the sins of the world, and by that gave all that believe in Him everlasting life.

1st Corinthians 15:42
So also is the resurrection of the dead, It is sown in corruption; it is raised in incorruption

1ˢᵗ Corinthians 15:43
It is sown in dishonor; it is raised in glory. It is sown in weakness and raised in power.

1ˢᵗ Corinthians 15:44
It is sown a natural body; It is raised a spiritual body. There is a natural body and a spiritual body.

1ˢᵗ Corinthians 15: 47
Adam the first man was made from the dust of the earth, earthly; While Christ the second man is the Lord from heaven.

1ˢᵗ Corinthians 15: 49
Just as we are now like Adam, the man of earth, so we will someday be like Christ the man from heaven.

Bishop Gilbert Earl Patterson said,

> "By Christ dying He took away sin. He was the ultimate sacrifice. By Christ being resurrected from the dead, He took away death and gave us everlasting life".

Dr. Creflo Dollar said,

> "I had no life before Jesus, for Jesus is my life line. Through Jesus you have peace, joy, love, wisdom, knowledge and understanding.

Bible Study # 18
From the teaching of Dr. Hillard
Input also by Anita Cameron

Iniquities

Iniquity is a commitment to sin, without shame, with strength and weakness.

A generation of sin passed down through another generation.

It is a weakness or a type of temptation that has been passed down from one generation to another.

Dr. Hillard stated,

"Iniquities can go from generation to generation (4 generations).

But, you can stop it at you."

Ex: Worshipping idols from generation to generation. An idol can be anything or anybody.

But you can stop it at you.

For ex:

>Grandfather went to jail for stealing or killing.
>Father also went to jail for the same things.
>Son goes to jail
>Daughter goes to jail.
>But you can stop it at you.

Ex:
    Grandfather's anger caused him to abuse his wife and family.
    Father's anger caused him to do the same thing.
    Son followed the same path.
    But you can stop it at you.

Ex:
    Parents addicted to or selling drugs.
    Children follow the same path too.
    But you can stop it at you.

Ex:
    Grandparents didn't believe in The Holy Trinity, Father, Son and the Holy Ghost.
    Children felt the same way.
    But you can stop it at you.

Because of the iniquities of the children of Israel, God did not let them get to the promise land until the third and fourth generation of those that disobeyed and tested Him.

Eventhough they had seen the glory of God before and after He had Moses lead them out of the land of Egypt, they still disobeyed God and tested Him.

Lamentations 5:7
Our fathers sinned and are no more, and we bear their punishment.

Numbers 14: 18
The Lord is slow to anger, abounding in love and forgiving sin and rebellion, yet He does not leave the guilty unpunished. He punishes the children for the sins of the father to the third and fourth generation.

Numbers 14:22
The Lord said, "Not one of the men who saw my glory and the miraculous signs I performed in Egypt and in the desert but who disobeyed me and tested me ten times.

Numbers 14: 23
Not one of them will ever see the land I promised on oath to their forefathers. No one who has treated me with contempt will ever see it.

Know matter what the iniquities are,

You can stop it at you.

Ezra 9: 13
And after all that is come upon us for our evil deeds, and for our great trespass, seeing that you our God has punished us less than our iniquities deserve, and has given us such deliverance as this.

Psalms 103:1
Blessed the Lord, Oh my soul, and all that is within me, bless His holy name.

Psalms 103: 2
Blessed the Lord, Oh my soul, and forget not all His benefits.

Psalms 103: 3
Who forgive all our iniquities; who healed all our diseases.

Psalms 103: 4
Who redeemed our life from destruction; who crowned us with loving kindness and tender mercies;

*Psalms **103: 10***
For He had not dealt with us after our sins; nor rewarded us according to our iniquities.

Psalms 103:13
Like as the father pitied His children, so the Lord pitied them that fear Him.

Psalms 103: 14
For He knows our frame; He remember that we are dust.

Psalms 103: 17
But the mercy of the Lord is from everlasting to everlasting upon them that fear Him, and His righteousness unto children's children.

Isaiah 53: 5
But Jesus was wounded for our transgressions, He was bruised for our iniquities; The chastisement of our peace was upon Him; and with His stripes we are healed.

1 Peter 2:24
Who His own self bare our sins in His own body on the tree, that we, being dead to sins, should live unto righteousness, by whose stripes we were healed.

The devil cannot make you do anything

The devil tries to put thoughts in your mine.

He knows the weakness in your family.

The devil tries to talk you into doing things but remember, the devil cannot make you do anything.

You have your own

a. Mine
b. Soul
c. Will
d. Emotions
e. Intellect

Therefore, you can stop it at you.

Praise The Lord.

Hallelujah

Bible Study # 19
From the teachings of
Rev. John Cherry

Unexpected Challenges

Rev Cherry said,

Everyone had a life before they met God.

They had feelings, desires and memories.

When they became saved and went up to the altar, all three went up with them, (their feelings, desires and memories)."

When they went back to their seat, their feelings, desires and memories went right back with them. They are not dead, but undercover. When challenged they resurface.

A person should not feel bad because they are 2 parts flesh and 1 part spiritual.

The success is when you are able to control those feelings, desires and memories.

For ex:

    a. We base future relationships on past memories, feeling and desires.
    b. A word can be spoken and bring or recall feelings or desires from the past.

Human element is chronic and lasting.

A mature saint must recognize the carnal from spiritual.

They must not take a response personal, but look at it as selfishness from that person. (You were in their way). If it hadn't been you, it would have been someone else.

Speaking of challenges

The unexpected challenges come from God. They exceed you mentally.

The expected challenges come from Satan. And all in God's word (Bible) tells you what to expect from Satan.

God lined all of it in the word (Bible).

An unexpected challenge was given to Moses.

Exodus 3:7
The Lord said to Moses, "I have surely seen the affliction of my people which are in Egypt, and have heard their cry by reason of their taskmasters (slave drivers). For I know their sorrows.

Exodus 3: 8
And I am come down to deliver them out of the hand of the Egyptians, and to bring them up out of that land unto a good and large land. A land flowing with milk and honey: Unto the place of the Canaanites, Hittites, Amorites, Perizzites, Hivites and Jebusites."

Moses thinking God is going to go in and deliver the Jews out of Egypt, but to Moses surprise God had chosen him.

who was slow of tongue(stammer).

Exodus 4: 1 Exodus 3:10
The Lord said to Moses, "come now therefore, and I will send you unto Pharaoh, that you may bring forth my people the children of Israel out of Egypt.

Exodus 3:11
And Moses said unto God, who am I, that I should go unto Pharaoh, and bring out forth the children of Israel out of Egypt?

Exodus 3: 12
And the Lord said, certainly I will be with you, and this shall be a token unto you, that I have sent you: When you have brought forth the people out of Egypt, you shall serve God upon this mountain.

Exodus 4:10
And Moses said unto the Lord, Oh my Lord, I am not eloquent, neither in the past nor since you have spoken unto thy servant. I am slow of speech and slow of tongue.

And Moses also said to God, but behold, they will not believe me, nor hearken unto my voice. For they will say, "the Lord has not appeared unto you."

Exodus 4:11
And the Lord said unto Moses, "Who gave man his mouth? Who makes him deaf or mute? Who gives him sight or make him blind? Is it not I the Lord?

Exodus 4: 12
Now go; I will help you speak and will teach you what to say."
Moses still feeling insecure said,

Exodus 4:13
"Oh Lord please send someone else to do it.

Exodus 4: 14
And the anger of the Lord was kindled against Moses. And The Lord said to Moses, "Isn't Aaron the Levite your brother? I know that he can speak well, and also, behold he is coming now to meet you: and when he see you he will be glad in his heart.

Exodus 4:15
And you shall speak unto him and put words in his mouth; and I will be with your mouth, and with his mouth, and will teach you what you shall do.

Exodus 4:16
And he shall be your spokesman unto the people. And he shall be, even he shall be to you instead of a mouth and you shall be to him instead of God.

In other words, "he will speak to the people for you, and it will be as if he were your mouth and as if you were God to him.

Exodus 4: 17
And God said take this staff in your hand so you can perform miraculous signs with it.

When God gives you unexpected challenges, He gives you all you need to accomplish the task.

Philippians 3: 14
I can do all things through Christ who strengthens me.

Bible Study # 20
From the teachings of:
Dr. Creflo Dollar
And my input, Anita Cameron

Trusting God

God said, "If you stay in that trust, I will anoint you."
No matter what happens in the natural, you have to trust in God.
To you it might look like nothings happening, but God's got it.
Remember, when your faith fails, you lose your confidence.
Whatever you place in God's hand it is secured.
When you put your children in God's hand, your children are secured.
When you put your life, business, and money in His hand, your life, business and money is secured.
Trust is at the advanced level, when you trust God at all things.
We have to learn how to rest in the Spirit.
Trust commands rest.
Know matter what happens you must trust in God.

When Moses was leading the Israelite people out of Egypt, and they saw that Pharaoh and his army where marching after them, they became terrified and cried out to the Lord. Then they began to question Moses by saying, "What have you done to us by bringing us out of Egypt?

*Exodus **14:12***
Didn't we say to you in Egypt, leave us alone, and let us serve the Egyptians? It would have been better for us to serve the Egyptians than to die in the desert.

Exodus 14:13
Moses answered the people Do not be afraid, Stand firm and you will see the deliverance the Lord will bring you today. The Egyptians you see today, you will never see again.

*Exodus **14:14***
The Lord will fight for you; you need only to be still.
We labor to enter into the peace of God and then divine intervention comes in.
The power of God is working in you and it is working for you.
Hallelujah
When circumstances come up, and you start feeling down, keep saying, the following:
The Power of God is working in me, and the power of God is working for me.
I trust in the Lord in all my heart, because He orders my steps.
Please don't let the devil turn off your switch.
Keep your switch on, by saying the power of God is working on the inside of me and for me. (Don't turn the switch off).
The Lord said "I will make an escape for you from all temptations."
You cannot be defeated and you will not quit.
God is for you, not against you.

Bible Study # 21
From the teaching of Dr. Charles Stanley
Input also by Anita Cameron.

The Will Of God

It is His purpose, plan and desire for our life.
Purpose for all humanity,
Plan for us individually,
Desire for us individually,
Only in the will of God you will have peace, comfort and prosperity.
There is no mistake or err in the will for God.
His plan for our life is perfect.
How do we discover what the will of God is?
Often it is a struggle for us to determine.
God's purpose is high an honorable.
His plan for us is the ultimate, so that we can reach our full potential.
God desire is for us to be happy.
If you don't want to know God's will for you, you will miss out on life.
God will show you His will.
It is the character of God.
He will give you directions to your life.
His responsibility is to tell us what to do, and we are to do what He tells us.

Apostle Paul is speaking to the Colossians.

Colossian 1: 9
For this reason, since the day we heard about you, we have not stopped praying for you and asking God to fill you with the knowledge of His will through all spiritual wisdom and understanding.

Colossian 1: 10
And we pray this in order that you may live a life worthy of the Lord and may please Him in every way: bearing fruit in every good work, growing in the knowledge of GOd.

Colossian 1: 11
Being strengthened with all power according to His glorious might so that you may have great endurance and patience, and joyfully

Colossian 1: 12
Giving thanks to the Father, who has qualified you to share in the inheritance of the saints of the kingdom of His Son.

Promises of God

Psalms 32:8
I will instruct you and teach you in the way in which you shall go: I will guide you with mine eye (watch over you).

David tells the Lord,

Psalms 16: 11
You have made known to me the path of life: you will fill me with joy in your presence and with eternal pleasures at your right hand.

Do you want to know the will of God?

It's the Word (Bible) of God.

The bible tells you and applies to everything in your life you need to know.

2 Timothy 3: 16
All scripture is God—breathed and is useful for teaching, rebuking, correcting and training in righteousness.

2 Timothy 3: 17
So, that the man of God may be thoroughly equipped for every good work.

Circumstances

Sometimes things happen that you don't understand, and sometimes things happen and you know why.

Always remember,
God is with His children moment by moment.

Romans 8: 28
And we know that all things work together for good to them that love God, to them who are the called according to His purpose.

Counseling

I am not talking about getting advice from someone; I am talking about getting counseling from a person that knows how to find the will of God.

1. You ask, "What do you feel God's Word says about my situation?
2. And what do you think God is telling me?"
   Then you go and pray on it.
   (Be very careful whom you ask for counseling.)

Conscience

Your conscience has to be trained on the word of God.
God has placed in everyone's conscience, knowledge, when we are walking in the Spirit.
Now when we keep doing something that isn't right our conscience leave us.
If we continue in sin, our conscience is seared.

1st Timothy 4: 1
Now the Spirit clearly speaks and says that in the latter times some shall depart from the faith, giving heed to seducing spirits and doctrines of the devils.

1st Timothy 4: 2
Such teaching come through hypocritical liars, whose conscience have been seared as with a hot iron.

The conscience must be trained in the word of God. The more likely you will walk in the truth.

Common Sense

Common sense is a gift of God.

1. We won't eat too much.
2. We won't drink, smoke or do drugs.

It is God's way of giving us and teaching us to ask; "What is my purpose for this?"
Common sense will never lead you to do something that is not the will of God.
God is in you to show you His will. He gives you the strong desire to do something.

Bible Study # 22
From the teaching of Charles Stanley
And input by Anita Cameron
From the readings of the Bible
King James Version (KJV)
And The New International Version (NIV)

Facing The Unknown

God is
Omnipotence (all power)
Omnipresent (Everywhere at all times)
Omniscience (knowing everything)

He knows all things, present and future.

Nothing goes beyond His knowledge.

God knows every circumstance.

KJV: Psalms 139: 1-4
O Lord, you has searched me, and known me.
You know my down sitting and mine uprising, you understand my thought afar off.
You compass my path and my lying down, and art acquainted with all my ways.
For there is not a work in my tongue, but, lo, O Lord, you know it altogether.

NIV; Psalms 139: 1-4
O Lord you have searched me and you know me.
You know when I sit and when I rise. You perceive my thoughts from afar.
You discern my going out and lying down; you are familiar with all my ways.
Before a word is on my tongue you know it completely.
In other words, you are never out of God's sight.

God knows everything about you.
He knows when you are sleeping and when you are awake.
He knows what you're going to say before you say it.
He is everywhere around you.
It is so wonderful and sometimes it's hard to take in.

Always remember He has all power.

What we don't know, He knows.
He knows what's going to happen.

He knows all of your intimate thoughts.
He knows all about what's going on in your family.

We don't have to know the future or the unknown as long as we have a Father that knows.

God plans good things for all His children.

God turns all things to good.

He takes the unknown things and makes it something awesome.
God causes all things to work together for good.

Sometimes things are going on in your life that you cannot explain or don't know how you are going to get through it. All of a sudden something happens and everything is worked out. You say to yourself, how did that happen or how did I get through this? Who was that person that just came and helped me by doing something or saying a word?

Sovereignty
Supreme Power

I know, no matter what's going on, God is in control.

KJV: Ephesians 1:4
According as He has chosen us in Him before the foundation of the world, that we should be holy and with out blame before Him in love.

God allows us to make choices, He can change it anytime, but He lets us choose.

Sometimes He lets us lie in sin so that we can recognize that He is all power.

God's presence is inevitable.

KJV: Romans 8:35
Who shall separate us from the love of Christ? Shall tribulation or distress or persecution or famine or nakedness, or perils; or sword?

KJV: Romans 8: 37,-38, 39
No, in all these things we are more than conquerors through Him that love us.

For I am persuaded, that neither death, nor life, nor angels, nor principalities, nor powers, nor things present, nor things to come,

Nor height, nor depth, nor any other creatures shall be able to separate us from the love of God, which is in Christ Jesus our Lord.

KJV: Romans 8: 32 & 33
If God be for us who can be against us.

He that spared not His own Son, but delivered Him up for us all, how shall He not with Him also freely give us all things.

He has the power to discipline us and to punish us.

What do you need in your life today?

God knows all our needs and He will provide you with all your needs.

KLV: Matthew 6: 8
Be not you therefore like unto them, for your Father knows what things you have need of, before you ask Him.

KLV: Matthew 6: 32 & 34
For your heavenly Father knows that you have need of all these things.

Take therefore no thought for tomorrow, for tomorrow shall take thought for the things of itself. Sufficient unto the day is the evil there of.

When you wake up in the morning, before starting out on your day, say to God these words.

God I thank you, and I know that you know all things, and you know in advance how my day will be and that you will take care of all my needs.

Thank you Father, you know all, you control all, and that I am walking in your presents. And that your love cannot be touched or changed; and that I stand and live in absolute confidence that you can handle my day, my night and my life forever; and that you can provide all things for me.

Children, don't worry or fret about things you don't know or
the unknown,
God knows.

Bible Study # 23
From the teaching of Dr. Creflo Dollar,
And input by Anita Cameron
From the readings of the Bible,
King James Version (KJV)
And The New International Version (NIV).

Walking In Authority

Exercise your authority.

Know when to practice your authority and when to pray.

John 14: 12
Jesus said "He that believes in me, the works that I do shall he do also: and greater works than these shall he do, because I go unto my Father.

John 14: 13
And whatsoever you shall ask in my name, that will I do, so that the Father maybe glorified in the Son.

Ask means Jesus is saying whatsoever you demand in my name.

Demand is His authority, and Jesus said, "I will do it."

Remember Jesus will not acknowledge sinful and illegal request.

John 16: 23
Jesus said, "In that day you shall ask me nothing, verily, verily I say unto you, whatsoever you shall ask the Father in my name, He will give it to you.

But, you must have confidence in the word of God.

You have to read the word and have confidence in it.

When confidence is resting in what you know, you have arrived.

Knowledge builds up confidence.

In your everyday life, knowledge builds up confidence.

Knowledge builds up confidence when you are laboring and exercising over the devil.

When you exercise authority over the devil in your own life,

then you can exercise authority over the devil in your children's and love ones life.

You must remember you cannot arbitrary cast devils out of other people.

A person has to want you to cast the devil out.

James 4: 7
Submit yourself therefore to God first, resist the devil and he will flee from you.

When you lay hands on the sick they will recover.

KJV Mark 16: 18
They shall take up serpents, and if they drink any deadly thing it shall not hurt them. They shall lay hands on the sick, and they shall recover.

NIV Mark 16: 18
They will pick up snakes with their hands; and when they drink deadly poison it will not hurt them at all; they will place their hands on sick people and they will get well.

When you carry this out, you are exercising your authority to do so.

Authority has nothing to do with feelings. You must exercise it.

You must keep laying hands on the sick because you have the authority to do so.

You must exercise your authority at all times.

I have authority whether I feel like it or not.

KJV 1 Peter 5:8
Be sober; be vigilant; because your adversary the devil, as a roaring lion, walks about seeking whom he may devour.

KJV 1 Peter 5: 9
Who resist steadfast in the faith, knowing that the same affliction are accomplished in our brethren that are in the world.

NIV 1 Peter 5: 8
Be self-controlled and alert. Your enemy the devil prowls around like a roaring lion looking for someone to devour.

NIV 1 Peter 5: 9
Resist him, standing firm in the faith, because you know that your brothers throughout the world are undergoing the same kind of suffering.

My God shall supply all my need.

Bible Study # 24
From the teaching of Dr.Creblo Dollar
And input by Anita Cameron
From the readings of the Bible,
King James Version (KJV).

Master Your Emotions

We cannot be emotionally ruled.

Emotions are feelings on the inside caused by pain or pleasure, trying to move us in certain directions.

3rd *John 1: 11*
Beloved, follow not that which is evil, but that which is good. He that do good is of God, but he that do evil, have not seen God.

If your thinking is aligned with the word, then your emotions will follow and move towards God's will.

You will not feel insecure on the inside, and you will not feel the need to control or have control over people.

If your thinking is in opposition to the word, then your emotions will move you in the direction away from God.

Satan is trying, through your emotions and your thinking, move you from the direction of God. (From the will of God.)

If you don't learn how to control your emotions, it will lead you into destructive behavior.

But you can take control of your emotions, by keeping forward; going toward the direction God wants you to go.

The problems of being emotionally removed, is moving you away from God.

The root of negative emotions is, having a sense of powerlessness.

Every negative emotion is our life consists of the following:

a. Anger about yourself.
b. Depression.
c. Feelings that you can't change.
d. Bad temper.
e. Condemnation.
f. Hopelessness.

The devil tries to tell you that you can not change,

1. Your circumstances.
2. Your personality.
3. Your weaknesses.

You have a God given right to change these things in your life.

You have authority over all these things.

You have authority over the devil.

You have authority over your circumstances.

Your have authority over your weakness.

You have authority over feeling a sense of powerlessness.

You have authority over sickness and diseases.

We tolerate things we don't need to tolerate.

It is our God given right to have authority over all things.

God gave authority to Adam over the Earth.

When Adam sinned by eating the fruit God told him not to eat, he lost his authority over to Satan.

Therefore, Satan had authority over the Earth.

When Jesus came down to the Earth, and made Himself the ultimate sacrifice for the entire world, He took back the authority and gave it to all the believers.

I have authority in the name of Jesus.

That person on your job or in your school that tries to intimidate you or make your life miserable, you can bind that spirit within them that's doing those things.

I want you to say 7 times, I have authority over the Earth. I have authority in the name of Jesus.

Bible Study # 25
From the teaching of Dr. Charles Stanley
And input by Anita Cameron.
From the reading of the Bible,
King James Version (KJV) and
The New International Version (NIV)

Anti-Christ

Anti-Christ is a liar, who denies Jesus as Christ.

Watch out and be aware of them.

The Davinci Code is Anti-Christ and even though we know it is fiction, some might believe the *Lie*.

For Jesus Christ is deity.

He is Divine, the Supreme Being and Holy.

His purpose was to redeem us.

These Anti-Christ are trying to make Jesus like a mortal man.

KJV 2nd John 1: 7
For many deceivers are entered into the world, who confess not that Jesus Christ is come in the flesh. This is a deceiver and an Anti-Christ.

KJV 2nd John 1: 8
Look to yourselves, that we lose not those things, which we have wrought (worked for), but that we receive a full reward.

KJV 2nd John 1: 9
Whosoever transgressed, and abide not in the doctrine of Christ, have not God. He that abide in the doctrine of Christ, he has both the Father and Son.

KJV 2nd John 1: 10
If there come any unto you, and bring not the doctrine, receive him not into your house, neither bid him God speed.

Ask a person if they believe that Jesus Christ came from heaven down to earth, and that in the flesh He suffered and died on the cross. By doing so He took away our sins. He went to hell and took back the key of life from Satan so that we now have everlasting life. He was resurrected back to heaven, and is now sitting on the throne on the right hand side of the Father.

There is only one answer and it is either yes or no.

If that person answers no, then that person is Anti-Christ and stay away from he or she.

Are you willing to compromise the truth to get alone with people? Do you feel you will hurt their feelings?

Either Christ is the way or it's your way. And if it is your way you will find yourself lost.

Anyone who accepts Jesus as his or her savior is saved.
Jesus came to reveal who God is.

His resurrection from the dead confirms that it is true.

If you deny Jesus Christ you have no assurance of anything, you will have to live your life away from the salvation of God, and when you die you have know idea where you are going.

All you have is that veil philosophy of life.

We as believers have *promises*, we have *eternal life with God*, we have the
Holy Ghost in our life and we are one day going to stand before Him in the likeness of Christ.

God warns us about the Anti-Christ. He warns us that their lies will turn believers of Jesus Christ into non-believers.

1st Peter 1:18
We were not redeemed with corruptible things, as silver and gold, from your vain conversation received by tradition from your fathers.

1st Peter 1: 19
We were redeemed with the precious blood of Christ as a lamb without blemish and without spots.

How do you protect yourself from Anti-Christ.

God has given us the Holy Ghost to concern us to identify err and truth.

The word of God explains things to us.

1. The Word of God is the Bible.
2. Jesus Christ is the Son of God.
3. Jesus Christ was deity in the flesh.
4. Salvation through Christ alone.
5. Christ dying on the cross is full payment for us.
6. The Holy Ghost dwells in every single believer.
7. Jesus Christ is coming back.
8. Our bodies will be resurrected.
9. The Holy Ghost has sealed us as a child of God.

To be saved you must believe that Jesus is deity and came in the flesh and died for our sins and was resurrected.

If you don't have Jesus, you have a vein nothing now and nothing after.

Remember the Anti-Christ's are children of the devil, and there is no truth in them.

2nd Corinthians 11:4
For if someone comes to you and preaches a Jesus other than the Jesus we preached, or if you receive a different gospel from the one you accepted, you put up with it easily.

Don't put up with it. Beware of deceivers.

Bible Study # 26
From the teachings of Dr. Charles Stanley
And input by Anita Cameron.
From the reading of the Bible,
King James Version (KJV) and
The New International Version (NIV)

Love In Its Highest Form

Love is from God, and love is God.

KJV 1st John 4: 7
Beloved let us love one another: For love is of God; and everyone that love is born of God and know God.

KJV 1st John 4: 8
He that loves not, know not God; for God is love.

KJV 1st John 4: 9
In this was manifested the love of God toward us, because God sent His only begotten Son into the world, that we might live through Him.

KJV 1st John 4: 10
Here in is love, not that we loved God, but He loved us, and sent His Son to be the propitiation (appease) for our sins.

KJV 1st John 4: 11
Beloved, if God so loved us, we ought also to love one another.

How God has declared His love for us

God's unselfishly giving Himself to bring goodness and blessing into our life.

God's love is commitment to you and me.

Even though, we don't deserve His love.

How has he expressed it in the past?

a. His creation.
b. He gave us dominion over all the earth.
c. He gave us rain, sunshine, snow, mountain trees etc.

We forget how beautiful God is.

God loved us before the foundation of the world.

KJV Ephesians 1: 4
According as He has chosen us in Him before the foundation of the world, that we should be holy and without blame before Him in love.

KJV Ephesians 1: 5
Having predestined us unto the adoption of children by Jesus Christ to Him according to the good pleasure of His will.

His continuously watch and care over us.

He manifested (clearly revealed) His love for us on the cross.

Romans 5: 8
But God commends His love toward us, in that, while we were yet sinners, Christ died for us.

There are two types of love unconditional and conditional.

The nature of God's love is unconditional.

There are no restrictions and no limitations; meaning no ifs or buts.

We on the other hand have conditional love for one another.

Conditional love means,

a. You have to measure up to expectation.
b. Will never say I love you unless you measure up on someone's expectation.

Conditional love creates,

a. Stress.
b. Being unsure.
c. Doubt.
d. Live with fear.
e. Never knowing whether you measure up or not.
f. You fear you're being cheated on.

We were brought up as children under conditional love. If we did well in school our parents showed us love.

But God has unconditional love for us even if we are doing something wrong.

Jesus loves you unconditionally. There are no restrictions or conditions.

But we have this projection that Jesus only loves us when we do certain things.

Unconditional love is difficult for us to believe, because to us,

a. It's unreasonable.
b. We've been taught wrongly.
c. We have guilt feelings

    Ex: How could God love me after what I've done?

d. Failures.

The same love that sent Jesus Christ to the cross to save us is the same God that loves you personally.

God has total unconditional love. His love for you cannot be changed no matter what your past consist of.

God does discipline us. He disciplines us because He loves us.

God's purpose for discipline is not punishment, but, for correction.

KJV John 3: 36
He that believes on the Son has everlasting life. And he that believed not the Son shall not see life; but the wrath of God abides on him.

God's wrath is God's deliberate punishment for sin, rebellion, and wickedness because He is angry with them.

You cannot separate the love of God and the justice of God.

His justice demands a punishment for sin.

God's judgment is for us to be rewarded for our works.

For the wicked, the degree of punishment they will receive.

God's nature and character is love and justice,

and, love and forgiveness for those who repent.

God does not send anyone to hell.

When people die without Jesus and they separate themselves from God by being rebellious, and defying God, and in their dying hour they curse God. Those are the ones that send themselves to hell.

God is a wise God, He loves us unconditionally but He knows mans character and He gave us all a mind to reason with.

If you love someone unconditionally, regardless of what they do you still love them.

It takes a commitment. You love them know matter what.

a. Sickness.
b. Or whatever changes are made.
c. You make no commands on them.

When two people love unconditionally, they will never have to worry about each other.

Bible Study # 27
From the teaching of;
Dr. David Jeremiah and additional
Input by Anita Cameron. From the bible
King James Version (KJV).

The Heavenly City

The heavenly city is the city that God is or has built for us in the 3rd heaven, and it is coming down.

11 times is Revelations we find the Word City. It is a city where we will live.

Revelations 3:12
Jesus said, "Him that over come will I make a pillar in the temple of my God, and he shall go no more out: and I will write upon him the name of my God, and the name of the city of my God Is New Jerusalem. Which come down out of heaven from my God: and I will write upon him my name".

John 14: 2
Jesus said "In my Father's house are many mansions, if it were not so, I would have told you, I go to prepare a place for you".

John 14:3
And if I go and prepare a place for you, I will come again, and receive you unto myself; that where I am, that you may be also.

Revelations 21: 1
John said "and I saw a new heaven and a new earth. For the first heaven and the first earth were passed away and there was no more sea.

Revelations 21:2
And I John saw the holy city, New Jerusalem, come down from God out of heaven prepared as a bride adorned for her husband.

The Dimension of the city

Revelations **21:15**
John said "and he that talked to me had a golden reed to measure the city, and the gates there of, and the wall there of.

Revelations 21:16
And the city lied foursquare, and the length is as large as the breadth: and he measured the city with the reed, twelve thousand furlongs. The length, breadth and the height of it are equal (1,377 miles).

Revelations **21: 17**
And he measured the wall there of an hundred and forty and for cubits according to the measure of man, that is, of the angel.

All the cities of the world are considered a village compared to the city God is dropping (descending) out of heaven.

This is a city whose builder and maker is God.

This city is the largest we have seen or will ever see (600 floors).

Revelations 21:3
John said "and I heard a great voice out of heaven saying. Behold, the tabernacle of God is with men, and He will dwell with them, and they shall be His people, and God Himself shall be with them, and be their God.

The description of the city

1. It's a Holy city.
2. It has pearly gates.
3. The foundation of the city is of precious stone.
4. The streets are made of Gold.
5. The Lamb (referring to Jesus) is the light.
6. Consist of the tree of life.
7. Consist of the river of life.

Revelations 21:18
And the building of the wall of it was of jasper: and the city was pure gold, like unto clear glass.

Revelations 21: 19
And the foundations of the wall of the city were garnished with all manners of precious stones. The first foundation was jasper; the second sapphire; the third a chalcedony; the fourth and emerald.

Revelations 20: 20
The fifth, sardonyrs; the sixth, sardurs; the seventh, chrysolyte; the eight, beryl; the ninth, a topaz; the tenth, a chrysoprasus; the eleventh, a jacinth; the twelfth, an amethyst.

Revelations 21: 21
And the twelve gates were twelve pearls; every several gates was of one pearl; and the street of the city was pure gold, as it were transparent glass.

Revelations 21: 22
And I saw no temple therein; for the Lord God almighty and the Lamb are the temple of it.

Revelations 21: 11
Having the glory of God: and her light was like unto a stone most precious, even like jasper store, clear as crystal.

Revelations 21: 23
And the city had no need of sun, neither of the moon to shine it: for the glory of God did lighten it, and the Lamb is the light there of.

Isaiah 60: 19
The sun shall be no more light by day; neither for brightness shall the moon give light unto you: but the Lord shall be unto you an everlasting light, and thy God thy glory.

1st Corinthians 2: 9
But as it is written, eyes have not seen, nor ears heard, neither has entered into the heart of man, the things, which God has prepared for them that, love Him.

Heaven is a magnificent place made by the hands of God.

God has made us real estate agents to bring people in.

Revelations 22: 1
John said "And he showed me a pure river of water of life, clear as crystal, proceeding out of the throne of God and of the Lamb.

Revelations 22:2
In the midst of the street of it, and on either side of the river, was there the tree of life, which bare twelve manner of fruits, and yielded her fruit every month: and the leaves of the tree was for the healing of the nations.

Psalms 46:4
There is a river, the streams where of shall make glad the city of God, the holy place of the tabernacles of the most High.

The gates are never closed. We will be able to go in and out.

Those that will not enter

Revelations ***21:8***
But the fearful, and unbelieving, an abominable, and murderers, and whoremongers, and sorcerers, and idolaters, and all liars shall have their part in the lake of fire and brimstone which is the second death.

Revelations 21: 27
And there shall in no wise enter into it any thing that defiled, neither whatsoever work abomination, or make a lie; but they which are written in the Lamb's book of life.

If you've never repented from sin, you will not enter into the city, you will be denied.

You must acknowledge your own sin and repent of your sin, and accept Christ as your Lord and savior, then your name will be written in the book of life and you will be a resident in the city of Jerusalem.

Grant Jeffrey—of Bible Prophecy Revealed stated "we will be ourselves in heaven and know and recognize each other, but it won't be with malice, jealousy or vanity. We will not have any illnesses of diseases. We will have quality time with each other. We will be able to travel faster than the speed of light to go anywhere in the universe we wish. Where it takes man presently 100,000 years to get to a planet, we will be able to explore places we've always wondered about by thinking about it and in an instance we are there.

Bible Study # 28
From the teachings of
Bishop G. E. Patterson and
Input by Anita Cameron, Bible
King James Version (KJV)

How To Get Your Prayers Answered

When you go to God in prayer you must know in your spirit that

1. God exists.
2. And that you must seek Him with diligence.
3. And you must go to His word.

God does not lie. If He said it, so shall it be.

Hebrew 11: 6
But without faith it is impossible to please Him: for he that come to God must believe that He is, and that He is a rewarder of them that diligently seek Him.

1st John 5: 14
And, this is the confidence that we have in Him, that if we ask anything according to His will, He hears us.

Will meaning it is a testament.

1st John 5: 15
And, if we know that He hear us, what so ever we ask, we know that we have the petitions that we desired of Him.

Prayer Is both Praise and Petition

First you must recognize who God is. (give Him praise).

Our Father Who Art In Heaven.

Psalms 34: 7
The angel of the Lord camped round about them that fear Him, and delivered them.

John 14:13
And what so ever you shall ask in my name, that will I do, that the Father may be glorified in the Son.

John 14: 14
If you shall ask anything in my name, I will do it.

How Do We Know We Are Praying In His Will?

John 15:7
Jesus said "If you abide in me. And my words abide in you, you shall ask what you will and it shall be done unto you."

Mark 11: 23
Jesus said "For verily I say unto you, that who so ever shall say unto this mountain be thou removed, and be thou cast in the sea; and shall not doubt in his heart, but shall believe that those things which he said shall come to pass; he shall have whatever he said".

Mark 11: 24
Jesus said "Therefore I say unto you, what things so ever you desire, when you pray, believe that you receive them, and you shall have them."

Mark 11; 25
Jesus said "and when you stand praying, forgive if you have ought against any; that your Father also which is in heaven may forgive your trespasses."

Mark 11:26
Jesus said "But if you do not forgive, neither will your Father which is in heaven forgive your trespasses.

Bible Study # 29
From the teachings of Pastor Bill Winston
And Pastor Duane Vanderklok.
Input by Anita Cameron, and using the
King James Version(KJV) of the bible.

Redeemed From Death

People have spent their whole life fearing death, and living in fear.

The fear of death and fear:

a. Is something that Satan places in your mind,
b. And are misquotes of the scriptures.

> Death is not from God, it is not a friend of Jesus and it's not a friend of yours.

> People are trying to live at the fear of death. They are fearful of going hiking, on cruises, flying in an airplane, taking over their neighborhood etc.

> People cannot enjoy life by fearing death.

1st John 5: 17
All unrighteousness is sin: and there is a sin not unto death.

1st John 5: 18
We know that who so ever is born of God sinneth not: but he that is begotten of God keeps himself, and that wicked one touched him not (Satan cannot touch you).

> We are sheep among wolves, and God knows the wolves are out there waiting to devour us, therefore God protects us.

> There is no such thing as an accident in God.

Therefore, put death on a shelf until its time for you to die.

Acts 28: 1 2
This is about how the apostle Paul as a prisoner and the crew that was on a ship sailing for Rome was shipwreck, and how all was saved (276 people) just as God had told Paul.

When they escaped the shipwreck, they came to an island call Melita. The people of the island were barbarous (uncivilized, lacking culture) and showed kindness: for they kindled a fire for them because of the present rain, and because of the cold.

Acts 28: 3
And when Paul had gathered a bundle of sticks, and laid them on the fire, there came a viper (a poisonousness snake) out of the heat and fastened on his hand.

Acts 28: 4
And when the barbarians saw the venomous beast hang on his hand, they said among themselves, no doubt this man is a murderer, whom though he has escaped the sea, yet vengeance suffer him not to live.

Acts 28: 4
And he shook off the beast into the fire, and felt no harm.

Paul did not fear death.

In the book of Daniel:
King Nebuchadnezzar demanded that the 3 Hebrew boys, Shadrach, Meshach, and Abednego fall down and worship an image of a gold idol. He had stated previously that who so ever refuse to fall down and worship the idol shall in the same hour be cast into the midst of a fiery furnace.

Shadrach, Meshach and Abednego refused to do so. They stated that they should bowl down to no other God, but the God of Abraham, Isaac and Jacob.

To put fear in them, he told them that they would be casted in the burning fiery furnace. He also asked them "who is this God that shall deliver you out of my hands?

Daniel 3:17
Shadrach, Meshach and Abednego, answered and said to the King, "If it be so, our God whom we serve is able to deliver us from the burning fiery furnace, and He will deliver us out of your hand, O King.

Daniel 3:18
But if not, be it known unto you, O King, that we will not serve your gods, nor worship the golden image, which you have set up.

King Nebuchadnezzar had the furnace heated seven times more than it was to be heated, and he commanded his most mighty men to put all three into the burning fiery furnace.

Daniel 3:23
And these three men, Shadrach, Meshack, and Abednego, fell down bound into the midst of the burning fiery furnace.

Daniel 3:24
King Nebuchadnezzar asked "Did not we cast three men bound into the midst of the fire? They answered and said to the King, yes.

Daniel 3:25
He answered and said, lo, I see four men loose, walking in the midst of the fire, and they have no hurt; and the form of the fourth is like the Son of God.

Because they did not fear death, they lived and the wicked one touched them not.
The fire had no power over them. When they came out of the fire their hair was not singed, neither was their coats, nor the smell of fire was on them.

The devil knows that if you stop fearing death and fear you will start to enjoy life.

With fear out of your life, you enjoy life.

WE must stop fearing.

1. The church controls you with fear.
2. The job controls you with fear.
3. Terrorism is using fear as a weapon.

A demon cannot touch you if you have no fear.

We have to get in a place where we have no more fear.

God Does Not Want Us To Live In Fear.

Adam fell from life to death. He left God as His father and became a son of Satan's.

Jesus came so that we can be born from death to life, from being son's of Satan to sons of God. Therefore, we have overcome fear of death.

Death is an appointment with death when you get ready.

Pastor Duane Vander Klok said, "that if you resist the devil he will flea from you.

You submit to God and God gives you authority spiritually to resist the devil.

Jesus defeated the devil in a flesh and blood body just as we have."

Hebrews 2: 14
For as much then as the children are partakers of flesh and blood, He also Himself likewise took part of the same; that through death He might destroy him that had the power of death that is the devil.

Bible Study # 30
From the teachings of Bishop G.E. Patterson
And input by Anita Cameron, Bible
King James Version (KJV)

Surrounded by enemies

Remember God delivers.

Psalms 3
David wrote this psalm when he was fleeing from his son Absalom.

In verse # 1
David expresses the shock and surprise to see the amount of enemies against him. You will find yourself surrounded by enemies.

Psalms 3:1
David said, "Lord, how are they increased that trouble me! Many are they that rise up against me.

In verse #1 and 2, David complaint is that the enemies are people with his son.

Psalms 3:2
Many there be which say of my soul, there is no help for him in God.

In verses 3 & 4,
David say's "God deliverance gives him confidence in God."

Psalms 3:3
David said "But thou, O Lord, art a shield for me; my glory, and the lifter up of mine head.

Psalms 3:4
David said "I cried unto the Lord with my voice, and He heard me out of His holy hill. Selah.

Verse 5 & 6
David's assurance of the Lord's protection.

Psalms 3:5
David said "I laid me down and slept; I awaked; for the Lord sustained me.

Psalms 3: 6
David Said "I will not be afraid of ten thousand of people that have set themselves against me round about.

Remember there is help in the Lord.

Table of Contents

1. Confronting Closed doors 125
2. Fasting 129
3. Wisdom 131
4. Look to the Lord Only 135
5. Living Godly in an ungodly age....................................... 139
6. God's Will for the prosperity 143
7. The ways of God... 146
8. The power of Thanksgiving 153
9. Salvation 156
10. Looking at Christmas through the eyes of others........... 160
11. The power of the mind and the battle of the mine 162
12. The God Class 165
13. Law of Confession 168
14. Remember Who Died for you 171
15. In a Father's Footsteps 176

Bible Study # 31
From the teaching of Dr. Charles Stanley
Input by Anita Cameron and the
King James Version (KJV)

Confronting Closed Doors

There are four reasons why doors are closed in your life.

1. Pure circumstances.
2. Something someone else does.
3. Satan
4. It's God who shuts the door.

Why does God close the doors on our life?

He closes the door

1. To protect us from making a mistake.
   a. He knows what's on the other side.
   b. God knows what we don't know.

   If we could see what He knows, we wouldn't want to continue through that door.

Proverbs 3:5
Trust in the Lord with all thine heart and lean not unto thine own understanding.

Proverbs 3:6
In all thy ways acknowledge Him and He shall direct thy paths.

He closes the door

2. To redirect us to a greater opportunity.

> When the Spirit of God comes He makes it clear.
>
> We must pray to God.
>
> We must listen to the prompting of the Spirit.
>
> The Spirit of God will sensitize your spirit.
>
> The prompting of the Spirit is urging our spirit to do something.
>
> Paul obeyed God and the gospel was spread all over the world.

He closes the door

3. To redirect us to greater fruitfulness.
4. To redirect us to greater satisfaction.

> God does mightier things in your life.
>
> Let your children see you respond to the Holy Spirit.

He closes the door

5. To redirect us to greater pain.

> Bleeding is preparation for the blessing when you obey the Spirit.

He closes the door

6. To test our perseverance.
7. To test our faith.
8. To equip us for the big opportunity to another door opening.
9. To delay us for something better.

> Our disobedience disqualifies us for opportunities in our life.

The wrong way to respond

1. You try to open the door yourself.
2. You try to open the door by manipulating circumstances (try to get someone else).

> God knows what's on the other side.

3. You become emotionally upset.
   a. You become hostile.
   b. You become angry.

4. You blame someone else.
5. Rebel against God.

The right way to respond

1. Wait upon God for further instructions.

> Wait until you hear from God.
> It is better to wait for God than to be disobedient.

Isaiah 64: 4
For since the beginning of the world men have not heard, nor perceived by the ear, neither have the eyes seen, O God, beside thee, what He has prepared for Him that wait on Him.

2. He is going to show us exactly what to do.

> Look for God's purpose for you.

3. Anticipate the opportunity He has for you.
4. Thank Him for protecting you from making the wrong decisions.
5. Be faithful where you are until God opens the door.

> You have read enough to keep you out of a whole lot of trouble, and make you a possible example to your family.

Don't always blame yourself for closed doors, because sometimes you think an opportunity was for you and you feel that you have missed it. God maybe has closed the door because He felt that it wasn't right for you.

Bible Study # 32
From the teachings of Dr. Charles Stanley
Input by Anita Cameron,
King James Version (KJV)

Fasting

When you fast you are to abstain from something for the purpose of seeking God.

a. Relationships
b. Food
c. Sex

A relationship with God that's what fasting is all about.

Whenever You Do Fast Instructions

a. You don't look like you're fasting.
b. You don't act like you're fasting.
c. You don't tell anybody.

Purpose of Fasting

Matthew **6:16**
Moreover, when you fast, be not as the hypocrites, of a sad countenance: for they disfigure their faces, so that they may appear unto men to fast. Verily I say unto you, they have their reward.

Matthew 6:17
But you, when you fast, anoint your head, and wash your face.

Matthew 6:18
That you appear not unto men to fast, but unto your Father which is in secret: and your Father, which sees in secret, shall reward you openly.

Fasting is not for persuading but for preparation.

Fasting for Preparation

When You Fast:

a. Your mind gets sharper (clearer).
b. Your desire to hear Him intensifies (to hear Him speak).
c. Preparations for cleansing (the will of God).

Whatever God surface in your heart, He will enable it to be.

Be sure your fasting is in private.

Fasting is motivating and yearning to know God's purpose in your life.

Genuine fasting is resending in humility.

Holy God, who loves you with His whole heart, is going to deal with you.

He is going to deal with sin.

He's going to tell you about you, and what you need to do.

If we don't fast, then you don't have time for God.

Bible Study # 33
From Anita Cameron,
Bible-King James Version (KJV)

Wisdom

The fear of the Lord is the beginning of wisdom.

Wisdom was with the Lord before the foundation of the world.

In Proverbs, Wisdom speaks.

Proverbs 8:22
The Lord possessed me (wisdom) in the beginning of His way, before His work of old.

Proverbs 8:23
I was set up from everlasting from the beginning, or ever the earth was.

Proverbs 8:24
When there were no depths, I was brought forth: when there was no foundation abounding with water.

Proverbs 8:25
Before the mountains were settled; before the hills was I brought forth.

Proverbs 8:26
While, as yet He had not made the earth; or the fields, or the highest part of the dust of the world.

Proverbs 8:28
When He established the clouds above: when He strengthened the foundation of the deep;

Proverbs 8:29
When He gave the sea His decree, that the waters should not pass His commandment; when He appointed the foundations of the earth,

Proverbs 8:30
Then I wisdom was by Him, as one brought up with Him: and I was daily His delight, rejoicing always before Him.

Proverbs 8:31
Rejoicing in the habitable part of His earth, and my delight were with the sons of men.

Proverbs 8:32
Now therefore hearken unto me, O you children, for blessed are they that keep my ways.

Proverbs 8:33
Hear instruction, and be wise, and refuse it not.

Proverbs 8:34
Blessed is the man that hears me, watching daily at my gates, waiting at the post of my doors.

Proverbs 8:35
For who so find me find life, and shall obtain favor of the Lord.

Proverbs 8:36
But he that sin against me wrongs his own soul: all they that hate me love death.

All people that hate wisdom love death.

Proverbs 9:10
The fear of the Lord is the beginning of wisdom and the knowledge of the holy, is understanding.

Job 28:28
And unto man He said, behold, the fear of the Lord that is wisdom, and to depart from evil is understanding.

Proverbs 10: 13
In the lips of him that have understanding wisdom is found. But, a rod is for the back of him that is void of understanding.

Proverbs 10:16
The labor of the righteous tended to life: The fruit of the wicked to sin.

Proverbs 10: 17
He is in the way of life that keeps instruction: but he that refused reproof err.

Proverbs 10:18
He that hide hatred with lying lips, and he that uttered a slander is a fool.

Proverbs 10:19
In the multitude of words there wanted not sin, but he that refrains his lips is wise.

Proverbs 10: 20
The tongue of the just is as choice silver. The heart of the wicked is little worth.

Proverbs 10: 21
The lips of the righteous feed many (meaning teaching others). But fools die for want of wisdom.

Proverbs 10: 22
The blessing of the Lord, it makes rich, and He adds no sorrow with it.

Proverbs 10:23
It is as sport to a fool to do mischief: but a man of understanding has wisdom.

Proverbs 10: 24
The fear of the wicked, it shall come upon him: but the desire of the righteous shall be granted.

Proverbs 10:27
The fear or the Lord prolongs days: but the years of the wicked shall be shortened.

Proverbs 10:28
The hope of the righteous shall be gladness: but the expectation of the wicked shall perish.

Proverbs 10:29
The way of the Lord is strength to the upright: but destruction shall be to the workers of inquity.

Proverbs 10:30
The righteous shall be removed: but the wicked shall not inhabit the earth.

Proverbs 10:32
The lips of the righteous know what is acceptable: but the mouth of the wicked speaks forwardness.

Proverbs 25:12
What man is he that fears the Lord? Him shall he teach in the way that He shall choose.

Proverbs 25:13
His soul shall dwell at ease; and his seed shall inherit the earth.

Proverbs 25:14
The secret of the Lord is the beginning of the knowledge, but fools despise wisdom and instruction.

Proverbs 1:5
A wise man will hear, and will increase learning; and a man of understanding shall attain unto wise counsels.

Bible Study # 34
By Anita Cameron,
King James Version (KJV) of the Bible.

LOOK To the Lord Only

How many times, when you look back over your life, have God brought you through?

How many times have you called on Him and trusted Him for something and everything went well?

I bet you can't count the many times He has blessed you.

Yet, many of us look to others instead of Him.

Many Christians reject God by seeking worldly leaders for advice rather than use their divine gift to seek the Lord. They put others on pedestals and acts as though their knowledge is above the knowledge of the Lord.

In 1st Samuel, the Israelites wanted a king to lead them. Even though God had brought them out of the land of Egypt, fed them food from heaven and gave them water from a stone. He fought their battles and gave them the best land on earth filled with milk and honey, where they would never have to worry about food, water or anything. The Lord God reigned over them as their King. A King that forgave them, served them, and loved them and they were free men. All they were asked to do was to obey the commandments.

Yet they wanted an earthly King.

1st Samuel 8:6
But the thing displeased Samuel, when they said, "Give us a King to judge us," and Samuel prayed unto the Lord.

1ˢᵗ Samuel 8:7
And the Lord said unto Samuel, hearken unto the voice of the people in all that they say unto you: For they have not rejected you, but they have rejected me, that I should not rein over them.

1ˢᵗ Samuel 8:8
According to all the works which they have done since the day that I brought them out of Egypt even unto this day, where with they have forsaken me, and served other gods, so do they also unto thee.

*1ˢᵗ **Samuel 8:9***
Now therefore hearken unto their voice: However protest solemnly unto them, and show them the manner of the King that shall reign over them.

1ˢᵗ Samuel 8:10
And Samuel told all the words of the Lord unto the people that asked of him a King.

1ˢᵗ Samuel 8: 11-18 Summarized
Samuel tells the people the manner of the King that shall reign over them. He informed them of how their sons and daughters would be utilized by the king as his servants, either in war, or as servants in his palace, and for his officers and family.

The prophet Samuel informed them that the king would take their fields, vineyards, their olive yards and even the best of them, and a tenth of their seeds to be given to his officers and servants. And he would take a tenth of their sheep.

Samuel also informed them that the king would take their own personal servants and put them to his work and all the people will be his servants including them and the freedom that they have will be no more.

Nevertheless the people wanted a king and refuse to obey the voice of the prophet Samuel.

*1ˢᵗ **Samuel8: 20***
They stated that we also may be like all the nations; and that our king may judge us, and go out before us, and fight our battle.

How many times have we refused to listen to the voice of the Holy Spirit that is within us?

We have often ignored the voice because we do not want to adhere to it. We would rather do it our way and do our will instead of God's will for us. Then when trouble comes or what we put into plan doesn't work out, we call crying to the Lord for help. All we had to do was to listen and wait.

When you need to make a decision, do you pray to the Lord Jesus for guidance or do you ask others?

When you feel that you are being mistreated on your job, at home etc., do you let vanity set in or do you pray to the Lord on the behalf of those persons?

How many times have you done things to belong even though you knew in your heart that it was wrong?

How many times do worldly things seem more important than praising the Lord?

How many times have you denied the Lord your God just to keep from being criticized by others?

When you find yourself in trouble and don't see no way out, or when you feel you are all alone and no one cares, do you know that the Lord's with you?

Yes the Lord is with you at all times. He doesn't run away from you when the going gets rough. He guides, teach and empower you through the Holy Spirit that's inside of you.

The Lord loves you more than you can conceive. He wants the best for you.

Please don't let this world tell you that you need anything other than the Lord. He takes care of all your needs and He will fight your battles when you are right. He will chastise you because you are His child and He loves you.

Therefore don't put other on a pedestal; they are human just like you. God created them, and God creates the air they breathe.

Remember we are all just passing through this life that God gave us and we are subject to be here for a certain amount of time.

Pastor Randy Morrison says that we are not a human bean, but a spiritual bean mastering the human experiences.

Pastor Bill Winston says you are not natural working in the spiritual system, you are spiritual working in the natural system.

While we are here always look to the Lord for everything.

1st Samuel 16:7
For the Lord see not as man see, for man look on the outward appearance, but the Lord look on the heart.

Bible Study # 35
From the teaching of Dr. Charles Stanley,
Input by Anita Cameron.
Bible, King James Version (KJV)

Living Godly In An Ungodly Age

In the Bible, the book of Titus 1: 5-16, the apostle Paul is writing to Titus, informing him that he must hold fast the faithful words that had been taught to him, thereby enabling him to convince the gainsayers. He writes, for there are many unruly, vain takers and deceivers, whose mouths must be stopped. Who subvert whole houses teaching things which shouldn't be taught, but they do it for filthy lucre's sake.

Paul tells Titus to rebuke them sharply, and tell the people not to give heed to the Jewish fables, and commandments of men that turn from the truth, because they are defiled, unbelieving, and nothing is pure. Even their mind and conscience is defiled, and they will profess that they know God, but in works they deny Him, Being abominable, and disobedient.

How will you live a godly life in a world that is getting darker?

The character of our society is:

1. *Secular*—Indifference to or rejection or exclusion of religion and religious considerations.
2. *Materialistic*—What they have and what can they get is all that matters.
3. *Immoral*—Sex is used to advertise everything.
4. Anti-Christian—
    a. They got prayer out of the schools and if they could they would try to stop prayer all together.
    b. A society that is rebellious against God.
    c. A society that degrades God.

People following and joining in to belong have stress and empty vain philosophy.

Only God can legitimately fill words in your life.

5. *Rampant Deceptions*—Empty vain philosophy. People are being deceived and after following these people their conscience will be seared.
6. *False Document*—2nd Timothy 4: 3

For the time will come when they will not endure sound doctrine; but after their own lusts shall they heap to themselves teachers, having itching ears.

2nd **Timothy 4:4**
and they shall turn away their ears from the truth, and shall be turned into fables.

The darker things get, the more the people of the light began to see darker,

What is a Key to living a Godly life

Titus 1:9
Holding fast the faithful word as he has been taught, that he may be able by sound doctrine both to exhort and to convince the gainsayers.

Hold fast means hold tight, do not drift away from the truth.

The Bible is the mind of God on printed pages

God's redeeming love for mankind is a guide for mankind.

The Bible has survived from generations to generations. Many have tried to destroy it by burning it. It's still here, and is the most sold book in the world and the best seller of all times. This is a book of love.

In spite of our weakness and sin, the Father sent to earth His only begotten Son to die for our sins.

The Bible is—Salvation, it tell us how to live godly, how to serve God, and it defends us and defends our beliefs that

Christ is living on the inside of us.

The Christian life is the Holy Spirit living in us to lift up Jesus.

The Power of His word

1. Leads us to salvation.
2. Seals our steps.
3. Seals our wisdom.
4. Lifts our burdens.
5. Bring us joy.
6. Gives us peace.

What brings peace is the promise of the word of God.

While you are reading a scripture you have read before, through the Holy Spirit, suddenly it brings peace to you.

It has a positive affect on the human body.

7. God's word is a healing.
8. Brings us back on track.
9. Gives us hope.
10. Enables us to grow.

God saves us, He doesn't condemn us.

We have to expose and rebuke false doctrine, because no one can update the wisdom of God.

All of us that have been saved know it's the power of God.

Only God can give us perfect guidance in our ways.

When we look at our society, things are getting darker. Therefore, we must cling to the word or we might drift.

To cling to the word of God

1. You must believe it.
2. Willing to apply it.
3. For your safety, get the bible in your heart, your mind and on your lips.

If you don't have Jesus, you don't have anything and you are nothing but a shadow and have been deceived by the devil.

When Reading the Word of God

1. Read it carefully.
2. Meditate on it daily.
3. Ask yourself, what does it means to me now in my life.
4. Study seriously (read it)
5. Believe it whole heartily.

> Do not set yourself up to be a judge of His word by believing some of it.

6. Apply it personally by claiming the Holy Spirit to teach you about the bible.
7. Obey it deliberately.

> When you obey His word, God enrich you.

8. Share it openly.

The consequences of drifting

1. You began to think the way the world thinks.
2. The world wins your affections.
3. Compromising your convictions, by starting to say, well if everybody else is doing it, it must be true, or something to do.
4. Dominate your conversation.
5. Redirect your focus from God.
6. Influence your dress.
7. Steals God's tithe.
8. Alters your schedule (Coming together to worship).
9. Feed your mind sensual thoughts.
10. Ruins your testimony.
11. You will not be walking in the power of the Holy Spirit.

> If you follow the Bible our guidebook, eventhough you will go through difficulties in your life, you will go through peacefully knowing that The Lord is with you and that you are loved.

Bible Study # 36
From the teaching of Dr. Joseph Ripley,
Input by Anita Cameron,
King James Bible Version (KJV)

God's Will For Your Prosperity

Like it or not the Bible is true.

We don't want the challenge of what the Bible says. We want what we want, and we want the Bible to conform to our way of thinking.

Deuteronomy 8:1
All the commandments which I command you this day shall you observe to do, that you
May live, and multiply, and go in and possess the land, which the Lord swore unto your fathers.

You have got to work with the system of God. If you lose your soul, earth is the only heaven you will know.

To be honest, to be true, rather than fake the seed of the up right shall be mighty in the earth.

Matthew 43:4
But He answered and said, it is written, that man shall not live by bread alone, but by every word that proceed out of the mouth of God.

2nd Timothy 2: 15
Study to show thyself approved unto God, a workman that needs not to be ashamed, rightly dividing the word of truth.

Everyone needs to study the word of God. You need real revelations.

We have been given power and authority over the devil. We rebuke the devil.

We come in the name of Jesus and in the blood of Jesus Christ.

We should live by the will of God and everything out of His mouth.

Romans 10:9
That if you confess with your mouth the Lord Jesus, and shall believe in your heart that God has raised Him from the dead, you shall be saved.

Romans 10: 10
For with the heart may believe unto righteousness and with the mouth confession is made unto salvation.

*Romans **10:13***
For whosoever shall call on the name of the Lord shall be saved.

Hebrew 1: 3
Who being the brightness of His glory, and the express image of His person, and upholding all things by the word of His power, when He had by Himself purged our sins, sat down on the right hand of the Majesty on high.

Isaiah 55: 11
So shall my word be that go forth out of my mouth: It shall not return unto me void, but it shall accomplish that which I please, and it shall prosper in the thing where I sent it.

The Lord does not make mistakes.

The mind of Christ has no Fear.

He knows when you are lying.

He knows you are greedy.

1ˢᵗ Corinthians 10: 9
Neither let us tempt Christ, as some of them also tempted and were destroyed of serpents.

1ˢᵗ Corinthians 10: 10
Neither murmurs you, as some of them also murmured, and were destroyed of the destroyer.

1st Corinthians 10: 13
There have no temptation taken you but such as is common to man; but God is faithful, who will not suffer you to be tempted above that you are able; but will with the temptation also make a way to escape, that you may be able to bear it.

Bishop Ellis said "Feed your faith and starve your doubt to death."

Bible Study # 37
From the teaching of Charles Stanley,
John Hagee, and input also made by
Anita Cameron.
King James and NIV.
Versions of the Bible.

The Ways Of God

The closer we get to God the more we see Him.

God wants us to know Him intimately. He wants us to know His heart and see His ways.

God uses ordinary things to accomplish the extraordinary things.

God knows far beyond of what we know. He knows the beginning and He knows the end.

Remember He has a purpose and plan for each of us.

The things God use

Starting a Genesis 37:
God used Joseph's brothers, who hated him, to sell him into slavery. When he was brought down to Egypt he was placed in Pharaoh's captain of the guard's house to serve him and his family. The Lord was with Joseph, and the captain of the guard found favor in him and made him overseer over his house. When Joseph would not let the captain of the guard's wife seduce him, she became angry and accused him of trying to seduce her. Joseph was then placed in prison.

The Lord was with him and showed kindness and granted him favor in the prison warden eyes. So the prison warden put Joseph in charge of all those held in prison. God had also given Joseph the gift of interpreting dreams. God used a man that was in prison with Joseph to remember that Joseph had the gift of interpreting dreams and he informed Pharaoh of Joseph's dream, because he had a dream that no one could interpret.

Joseph interpreted Pharaoh's dream saying that for seven years it would be great plenty throughout Egypt and after the seven years there would be seven years of famine. Pharaoh put Joseph over all the land of Egypt. And by Joseph being in charge he saved up store houses of grain to not only feed all the people of Egypt for the seven years but also his father, brothers and their offspring during the famine. At his request his Father, brothers and their offspring moved to Egypt where food was plentiful. Joseph was well known and respected.

Starting from Exodus 1:6

After Joseph, his brothers and that generation died. There had arisen a new king over Egypt, which didn't know Joseph. The king made a decree that all Hebrew boy children born should be killed, because he feared the Hebrews had grown so much in numbers and that they might join with the enemies and fight against them. God used a wicker basket to hide and save Moses, and He used the daughter of Pharaoh to raise Moses as her son.

God used Moses to bring the Hebrews out of Egypt and He used Pharaoh to deny them leaving Egypt, even when the plague of blood, frogs, lice flies, disease on beasts, boils, hail, locust, darkness and Passover; for when the first born would die, unless the blood of the lamb was placed on the tops and the two side post of the door frame of the house.

When Pharaoh finally let the Hebrews leave Egypt, he had a change of mind and decided to go after them to kill them, but God opened the Red Sea and let all the Hebrew go through and drowned the Egyptian soldiers. All knew then that God had the power.

What do you see in your life?

God does not make unimportant people. We don't believe we are important. We often say, God can't or won't use me.

God is waiting for you to want to be used by Him.

You can't run from God. God sees all things, knows all things, all presence of all things are in His presence.

You try running from God and you will run right into a storm.

Starting at Jonah 1: 1

The Lord came to Jonah and said arise go to Nineveh, that great city, and cry against it; for their wickedness has come before me.

But Jonah rose up to flee unto TarsHish from the presence of the Lord. He felt he could hide from the Lord. The Lord prepared a great fish to swallow up Jonah, and

Jonah was in the belly of the fish three days and three nights. He prayed to the Lord and when the Lord had the whale release him, he did what the Lord said.

God accomplished through Jonah in spite of his attitude.

Have you found yourself running away from God and feel you are doing fine by yourself?

Well a storm is coming.

If God has a purpose for you, in spite of your attitude He will see that you accomplish what He has in store for you.

In the Book of 1st Samuel Chapter 16 & 17

God used David a child to accomplish the plan He had for him. Goliath the giant was taunting the people of God and the people were afraid of him. In those days it was hand to hand combat and it was very bloody.

God took a simple stone in the hand of a young boy David and Killed Goliath.

If God can use a stone, He can use you.

Most people miss the best opportunity of God's purpose for them because they feel they don't have anything God can use.

The Lord is listening for you to say, God whatever you want me to do, and I surrender my life to you. All to Jesus I trust in Him.

When you look over your life you'll see He was there and He's still there.

Sometimes we say, "Lord now I see what you were doing."

God knows what the outcome is going to be.

Knowing Gods Ways

*Psalm **81: 10-16***
I am the Lord your God. Who brought you up out of Egypt. Open wide your mouth and I will fill it.

But my people would not listen to me; Israel would not submit to me.

So I gave them over to their stubborn hearts to follow their own devices.

If my people would listen to me, If Israel would follow my ways, how quickly would I subdue their enemies and turn my hand against their foes!

Those who hate the Lord would cringe before Him, and their punishment would last forever.

But you would be fed with finest of wheat; with honey from the rock I would satisfy you."

We here in this country walk in our own way because it is all about wanting prosperity. But do we really get it?

You might feel that you have prosperity, but do you have peace, joy, unconditional love, contentment, and security?

When you walk in God's way, you have all the above.

His way is the best way. No matter what, He has something better for you.

Sometimes we think because He allows trouble to come in our lives, He doesn't love us or He has forgotten about us. You must remember He has a plan and purpose for our life, and that's just another step for us to take to show how much we trust in Him.

1. Walking in His way is the pathway to success.
2. When you walk in His way He demonstrates His awesome power.

How do we know His Way?

Isaiah 55:8
The Lord said, "For my thoughts are not your thoughts, neither are your ways my ways.

Isaiah 55:9
As the heavens are higher than the earth, so are my ways higher than your ways and my thoughts than your thoughts.

Psalm 139:6
Such knowledge is too wonderful for, too lofty for me to attain.

Romans 11:33
Oh, the depth of the riches of the wisdom and knowledge of God. How unsearchable His judgments, and His paths beyond tracing out.

Romans 11:34
Who has known the mind of the Lord? Or who has been His counselor?"

Romans 11:35
Who has even given to God, that God should repay Him?

Romans 11: 36
For from Him and through Him and to Him are all things. To Him be the glory forever, Amen.

You and I cannot understand the knowledge of God, only what He reveals to us.

If you don't have the Holy Spirit inside of you, you will not know the truth.

Deuteronomy 29:29
The secret things belong to the Lord our God, but the things revealed belong to us and to our children forever, that we may follow all the words of His law.

Walking in His way, there are no difficulties, He stabilizes you.

Benefits of walking In God's Way

1. Intimacy with God.
2. We get His viewpoint (we began to see things His way).

Bible Study # 38
From the Teachings of Dr. Charles Stanley,
Input by Anita Cameron.
Bible, King James version (KJV) and
The New International version (NIV).

The Power of Thanksgiving

We must thank God everyday and in every way we can.

Psalm 69:30-31
I will praise God's name in song and glorify Him with thanksgiving. This will please the Lord more than an ox, more than a bull with his horn and hoofs.

Romans 1:20
For since the creation of the world God's invisible qualities, His eternal power divine nature, have been clearly seen, being understood from what has been made, and so that men are without excuse.

If you want to be enlightened, you must thank God for the things you have and for what you understand.

Thanksgiving will bring you into enlightenment.

When you are unthankful, you become darker and darker in spirit.

Thankfulness is light. Things you didn't know will be revealed to you and you will gain knowledge.

Being ungrateful could bring lack in your life.

Being grateful can expand your life.

Luke 17:11-14
Now on the way to Jerusalem, Jesus traveled along the border between Samaria and Galilee. As He was going into a village, ten men who had

leprosy met Him. They stood at a distance, and called out in a loud voice, Jesus, master, have pity on us. When He saw them, He said "go, show yourselves to the priests," and as they went they were cleansed.

Luke 17: 15-17
One of when saw he was healed, came back praising God in a loud voice. He threw Himself at Jesus feet and thanked Him and he was a Samaritan.

Jesus asked, "were not ten cleansed? Where are the other nine? Was no one found to return and give praise to God except this foreigner? Then He said to him, "Rise and go; your faith has made you well.

How many times have we called on the Lord to save us or to help us with something, and as soon as we see ourselves free and clear we forget about where our help came from. It came from the Lord, and yet we forget to thank Him, and praise Him everyday.

To glorify God, you give Him thanks.

Use thanksgiving, for challenging situations to come out right.

David's Prayer of Thanksgivings

1st Chronicles 16:23-31

Sing to the Lord, all the earth: proclaim His salvation day after day. Declare His glory among the nations, His marvelous deed among all people.

For great is the Lord and most worthy to be praised. He is to be feared above all gods. For all the gods of the nations are idols.

The Lord made the heavens. Splendor and majesty are before Him; strength and joy in His dwelling place. Ascribe to the Lord, O families of nations, ascribe to the Lord's glory and strength, and ascribe to the Lord the glory due His name. Bring an offering and come before Him; worship the Lord in the splendor of His holiness.

Tremble before Him, all the earth! The world is firmly established; it cannot be moved. Let the heavens rejoice, let the earth be glad; let everyone that has breath praise the Lord and say "the Lord reigns"

1st Chronicles 16:34
Give thanks unto the Lord for He is good and His mercy and love endures forever.

Praise the Lord.

Bible Study # 39
From the teaching of Dr. Charles Stanley
Input by Anita Cameron. King James Version (KJV)
And New International Version (NIV)

Salvation

We have been redeemed.

Jesus, who made the heaven and earth, came down from heaven and paid the sin debt in full. The Father laid upon Jesus all the sins of the world.

John 1: 1-4
Jesus was with God in the beginning, through Him all things were made; without Him nothing was made that has been made. In Him was life, and that life was the light of men.

Eventhough Jesus made the earth, He came down to earth, born from a virgin, without sin. He could not come to earth through sin because He being holy came to earth to take away sin.

He lived an incorruptible life on earth.

John 1:10
He was in the world and though the world was made through Him, the world did not recognize Him.

John 1:12
Yet to all who received Him, to those who believed in His name, He gave the right to become children of God.

John 1:13
Children born not of natural descent, nor of human decision or a husband's will, but born of God.

John 6: 35-40
Jesus said "I am the bread of life. He who comes to me will never go hungry, and he who believes in me will never be thirsty. But as I told you, you have seen me and still you do not believe. All that the Father gives me will come to me, and whosoever come to me, I will never drive away. For I have come down from heaven not to do my will but to do the will of Him who sent me. That I shall lose none of all that He has given me, but raise them up at the last day. For the Father's will is that everyone who looks to the Son and believe in Him shall have eternal life, and I will raise them up at the last day.

John 6: 44
No one can come to me unless the Father who sent me draw Him, and I will raise Him up at the last day.

Until the Holy Spirit transpires in your life you will not be saved.

To Be Saved

1. You must understand who Jesus is. He is our redeemer; He laid His life down to save our souls. You must believe the word of God.
2. The action of repentance must take place. (I will change because I believe in Him).
3. You must genuine truly believe that you are a new creature, and that Jesus has atoned for all your sins and the sins that you will commit, pass, present and future.

He made it possible for everyone to be saved. Our responsibility is to trust in Him. By mercy He saved us from our sins.

This does not mean that you can go on doing the same sins over and over and it's Ok. One thing for sure when you trust and believe in Jesus, the Holy Spirit will guide you and let you know that you are doing something you are not surpose to be doing and your conscience will make you confess your sins. You will pray to the Lord for forgiveness and you will stop committing that sin.

When you pray to the Lord and confess your sins sincerely, He will forgive you and wipe away your sins never to be remembered.

But, Satan comes around to remind you of your past and do all he can to trap you back into doing those things again. Then if you keep remembering your past, you will start doubting the power of the Lord to wipe away your sins never to be remembered. You will start thinking there is no hope.

That's why you must keep in your mind and heart that Jesus paid the price for all our sins, no matter what you have done before, when you confess your sins to Jesus and believe in Him, all of your sins are forgiven and never to be remembered in heaven.

That's why we pray to the Lord for forgiveness and praise Him daily. We ask the Lord to forgive us, restore our fellowship with Him and to keep us from the lust, the unjust, corrupted and vile world, sickness, angry and negative people.

He orders that we ask for forgiveness and be cleansed so that we can stay in the light.

Before anyone is saved they are separated from God. They are in darkness, empty and lust of the flesh. The mind of a natural man does not relate to the Holy God.
Unless you have the Holy Spirit in you, you are in darkness and will be dealing with all types of evil spirits, such as jealous spirits, unforgiving spirits, angry spirits etc.

That why it's important to say this prayer everyday.

Matthew 6: 8-15

Our Father who are in Heaven
Hallowed be your name.
Your kingdom come.
Your will be done.
On earth as it is in heaven.
Give us this day our daily bread.
And forgive us our debts
As we forgive our debtors
And lead us not into temptation

But deliver us form the evil one.
For thine is the kingdom,
the power and the glory forever,
Amen

The first part of the prayer, you are praising God, knowing that He is Holy and have all power.

This prayer takes care of your daily needs when you say give us this day our daily bread.

When you ask for forgiveness you must forgive those who have trespass against you. Then the Father will forgive you.

A personal or intimate relationship with someone that has sinned against you or has hurt you, you must forgive them and leave everything in God's hand. No matter how deeply you have been hurt, if you are a believer in Christ, you must forgive.

When you pray to lead you not in to temptation and deliver you from the evil one, you are praying to the Lord to keep you from sin and to help you recognize Satan.

Remember that the Lord saved you in one act. He forgives you for your daily sins and if you confess your sins, eventually you will become closer to God and recognize when Satan is trying to temp you, and you will say, "No, I am not going that route anymore. I am a child of the living God, saved by grace. I am redeemed."

Bible Study # 40
From the teaching of Rev Vernon King
Input also by Anita Cameron
Bible: New International Version (NIV)

Looking At Christmas Through The eyes of another

God rewards us sometime by having us look through the eyes of others.

When you look through the eyes of others, your situation doesn't look to bad.

Stop complaining because there is somebody who would love to be in your shoes.

Every now and then we should look at life through the eyes of others.

Look through the eyes of a homeless person:

No home means they don't have a bed to lay their head down on. In the winter they have no heat. In the summer they have no air condition. Food is limited.
A bath is out of the question and whatever they have they must keep a close eye on it. Family gatherings are something never though of. Personal hygiene is forgotten.

Look through the eyes of the American troops that are stationed in Iraq:

Imagine having no idea when your last day will be. And you are placed in a strange country away from family, with snipers constantly trying to kill you.

Look through the eyes of a blind person, or a child being molested, or a single mother with children without a job or means to support them.

Look through the eyes of a policeman whose life is always on the line. Everyday when he leaves his home and family he's not sure of his return.

I remember when my grandmother told me about the story of the person who was complaining bout the shoes they had to wear when all of a sudden a person passed by without feet.

The Lord has been so good to us. We have so much to be thankful for. We must praise and thank Him everyday.

Some people cannot look through the eyes of others because it's all about them. They could care less about how others are doing or feeling.

2nd Timothy 3: 1-4
There will be terrible times in the last days.
People will be lovers of themselves, lovers of money, boastful, proud, abusive, disobedient to their parents, ungrateful, unholy, without love, unforgiving, slanderous, without self-control, brutal, not lovers of the good, treacherous, rash, conceited, lovers of pleasure rather than lovers of God.

Those people who cannot look through the eyes of others are impatience, selfish,
Unforgiving and they are never peaceful and contented. They always want to be in control of others.

But when you look through the eyes of others it will make you see how blessed you are.

Bible Study # 41
From the Teaching of Rev. Ellis of Detroit, MI
Input also by Anita Cameron.
Bible King James Version (KJV)

The Power of the Mind and the Battle of the Mind

The Lord said, "If you love me keep my commandments."

Romans 12: 2
And be not conformed to this world: but be you transformed by the renewing of your mind, that you may prove what is good, and acceptable, and the perfect will of God.

The mind is a terrible thing to waste.

The mind is powerful and full of possibilities. The ability of the mind is full of positions, promises, productivity and most of all full of power.

God gave man a mind.

When God made Adam, He gave him a mind. He didn't go to school. God gave him the power to do task.

There are more than 200 versus throughout the Bible about the mind.

Genesis 1:6
And the whole earth was of one language, and of one speech.

Everyone spoke the same language. God gave everyone a mind to hear and to be able to repeat what he or she heard and to reason.

Genesis 1: 2
And it came to pass, as they journeyed from the east, that they found a plain in the land of Shi-nai; and they dwelt there.

Genesis 1: 3
And they said one to another, go to, let us make brick, and burn them thoroughly. And they had brick for stone, and slime had they for mortar.

Genesis 1: 4
And they said, go to, let us build us a city and a tower, whose top may reach unto heaven: And let us make us a name, lest we be scattered abroad upon the face of the whole earth.

Just imagine to yourself how these people without any schooling and probably without the knowledge of how to build yet, their minds were able to do so.

Sometimes when using our mind and what we accomplish is not pleasing to God, that's why it's better first to confer with Him through prayer.

Genesis 1: 5
And the Lord came down to see the city and the tower, which the children of men built.

Genesis 1: 6
And the Lord said, behold, the people is one, and they have all one language; and this they begin to do. And now nothing will be restrained from them, which they have imagined to do.

Genesis 1:7
Let us go down, and there confound their language, that they may not understand one anther's speech.

A mind is very powerful and it can be the cause of making and doing a lot of wonderful things and a lot of evil things.

The more you use your mind in utilizing God's Word, the more you will be fulfilled.

Satan is always trying to overcome your mind. He tries to intimidate you into doing things against the will of God. He tries to confuse you by tempting you. He has watched an observed you and know your weaknesses.

Praise be to God our Lord and savior Jesus. Through His resurrection we were given the power to defeat the devil. We have been given the power to recognize his presents. Therefore when we know he is trying to persuade us in doing something against the will of God, we say in the name of Jesus or in the blood of Jesus, get behind me Satan.

The more you don't fall into his trap, the more he'll start leaving you alone.

God gave our minds to us and that separates us and makes us more powerful than any other beast on the earth.

If you notice, God gave you a mind for your own reasoning and decision making.

He is always there when you need guidance from Him through the power of the
Holy Spirit

Bible Study # 42
From the teaching of Rev. Bill Winston
Also input by Anita Cameron,
Bible: King James Version (KJV)

In The God Class

Matthew 21:21
Jesus answered and said unto them, verily I say unto you If you have faith, and doubt not, you shall not only do this which is done to the fig tree, but also if you shall say unto this mountain, be thou removed, and be cast into the sea, it shall be done.

Matthew 21: 22
And all things, what so ever you shall ask in prayer, believing, you shall receive.

Matthew 17:20
And Jesus said unto them, because of your unbelief: for verily I say unto you, if you have faith as a grain of a mustard seed, you say unto this mountain, remove hence to yonder place; and it shall remove; and nothing shall be impossible unto you.

No more limit. Stop thinking you can't do something.

Philippians 4:13
I can do all things through Christ which strengthens me.

Mark 9:23
Jesus said unto him, If you can believe, all things are possible to him that believes.

Every demon must bow down to the face of righteousness.

God is in us, doing the supernatural.

He is operating through us.

Psalms 115:14
The Lord shall increase you more and more, you and your children.

We are spiritual people dealing with human experiences. If you put God's word in your mouth and feed His word in your heart, you are not only going to speak like God, you are going to start walking, speaking, talking like God. I am a child of God imitating my Father.

Psalms 34:1
I will bless the Lord at all times; His praise shall continually be in my mouth.

Romans 10: 6
But the righteousness which is of faith speaks on this wise, say not in thine heart, who shall ascend into heaven? (That is, to bring Christ down from above).

Romans 10: 7
Or, who shall descent into the deep? (That is to bring up Christ again from the dead).

Romans 10:8
But what said it? The word is nigh you, even in your mouth, and in your heart. (That is the word of faith, which we preach).

Romans 10: 9
That if you shall confess with your mouth the Lord Jesus, and shall believe in your heart that God has raised Him from the dead, and then you shall be saved.

Oh magnify the Lord with me.

You can believe things with your heart, you can never believe with your head.

The Lord said, when you pray, if you believe you receive it, you will.

Psalms 102:13
Thou shall arise, and have mercy on Zion; for the time to favor her, yes, the set time, is come.

Glory to God our time is now.

Get on the Word of God.

The key is walking by faith.

Psalms 115: 14
The Lord shall increase you more and more, you and your children.

This is your year of more.

Bible Study # 43
From the teaching of Pastor Bill Winston,
Input also by Anita Cameron.
King James Version (KJV) Bible

Law of Confession

1st *John 1: 9*
If we confess our sins, He is faithful and just to forgive us our sins and to cleanse us from unrighteousness.

There are four confessions of sin

1. There is an unforgiving sin and that sin is when you do not believe in Jesus. That He is the only begotten Son of the Father, sent to earth to die for our sins. He went to hell and took the key of life back from Satan who had taken it from
    Adam, so that now we can have everlasting life. He was resurrected, went back up to heaven and is now on the right hand side of the Father on the throne of glory.

2. Confessions when you bring back up your old sins. When you do that you are weakening your spirit and Satan wants you to weaken your spirit. The more you weaken your spirit the more your faith in God is decreased.

3. Confession of the believer to say the same things that God says. In all our ways acknowledge Him and He will set our ways positive.

Romans 10:10
For with the heart man believe unto righteousness; and with the mouth confession is made unto salvation.

Sure you must confess your sins to the Lord but there is another confession and that's

4. Confession above what is negative.

We are three: spirit, soul and body.

Once you get born again you have to rise above negativity.

The words that you confess out of your mouth are how far you see yourself.

How about confessing out of your mouth that you are strong, and that you have power from the Father and our Lord Jesus to achieve and do far beyond of what's expected, because of how you see yourself before you say it.

When you get a headache you have to see yourself without a headache and confess it out of your mouth saying I do not have a headache.

Once you get born again, you can say it before you see it.

For you to please God you have to renew your mind.

Romans 12: 1
I beseech you therefore, brethren, by the mercies of god, that you present your bodies a living sacrifice, holy, acceptable unto God, which is your reasonable service.

Romans 12: 2
And be not conformed to this world: but be you transformed by the renewing of your mind, that you may prove what is good, and acceptable and perfect will of God.

John 6:63
It is the spirit that quickened; the flesh profited nothing; the words that I speak unto you, they are spirit, and they are life.

Our words are spirit. Your spirit is a bag that holds words.

You have the power to say I am not sick; I am well. When you say it mean it.

Sickness is evil. So don't let Satan take away your power.

You and I should be walking as kings in the earth.

Words are the most powerful things.

There is a spiritual law and there is a natural law.

You must have confidence in your word.

Say what you mean and mean what you say.

I am somebody. I am a child of God and my Father owns everything. He has riches far above all and all power is in His hand.

Therefore believe what you say and it will come too past.

The devil wants your mouth and God wants your mouth.

We have not made the connection as to what we say out of our mouth is what will come to past.

God wants you to speak up things not tear things down.

Let Positive and good things come out of your mouth.

Bible Study # 44
By Anita Cameron
King James Version (KJV)
Lost Books of the Bible

Remember Who Died For You

When heaven and earth was created Jesus was there.

John 1:1
In the beginning was the Word (Jesus) and the Word was with God and the Word was God.

John 1:1
The same was in the beginning with God.

John 1:3
All things were made by Him; and without Him was not anything made that was made.

Genesis 1:26
And God said "Let us make man in our own image, after our likeness: and let them have dominion over the fish of the sea and over the fowl of the air and over the cattle and over all the earth, and over every creeping thing that creeps upon the earth.

God gave man authority and power over everything, but our authority was taken away because of Adam and Eve's sin.

When God made Adam out of the dust of the earth and breathed life into Him, he became a living soul. Eve was taken from Adam's rib and she was called woman.

They lived in the sweet smelling always day light Garden of Eden. They were to live forever. They had no worries at all.

The heavens were so close they could see the Angels praising God. They had pure water, fruits and excellent health. They had everything they needed and more.

The Lord told them they could eat any fruit except for the fruit of the tree in the mist of the garden.

Genesis 3:3
God said "You shall not eat of it neither shall you touch it, lest you die.

Eve let the serpent persuade her to eat of the fruit and she persuaded Adam to do the same.

Genesis 3:23
Therefore the Lord God sent him (Adam) from forth from the Garden of Eden to till the ground from whence he was taken, a land rough and full of trouble.

That was the fall of man. Because they used their own free will to transgress and not keep God's commandments.

Adam and Eve were taken out of paradise into a hard life, because they listen to Satan.

V111: 1

Adam wept and said "O Lord, when we dwelled in the garden, and our hearts were lifted up, we saw the angels that sang praises in heaven, but now we do not see as we were use to do. When we entered the cave all creations became hidden from us.

Then God the Lord said unto Adam, "When you were under subjection to me, you had a bright nature within you. And for that reason you could see things afar off. But after your transgression your bright nature was withdrawn from you and it was not left to you to see things afar off, but only near at hand; after the ability of the flesh; for it is brutish."

The Lord said, "I commanded you concerning the tree, that you should not eat thereof, yet I knew that Satan, who deceived himself would also deceive you.

The wicked Satan, who was thrown out of heaven because he tried to take over heaven, was the one who made the tree appear pleasant in Eve's eyes.

So I made known to you by means of the tree, not to come near him. And I told you not to eat of the fruit, nor taste of it, nor yet sit under it, nor to yield to it.

Had I not been and spoken to you O Adam concerning the tree, and had I left you without a commandment, then you had not sinned.

But I commanded you, and warned you and you did fall, So that my creatures cannot blame me; but the blame rests on them alone."

The Lord said, "I have made the day for you and your children after you, for them to work and toil therein, and I have made the night for them to rest in it from their work."

XIV: 1

Then Adam said to God "O Lord, take my soul, and let me not see this gloom any more. Or remove me to some place where there is no darkness.

XIV: 2

But God the Lord said to Adam, "Verily I say unto you, this darkness will pass from you. Everyday I have determined for you, until the fulfillment of my covenant. When I will save you and bring you back again into the garden, into the abode of light you long for. Where there is no darkness. I will bring you to it, in the Kingdom of Heaven."

XIV: 3

Again God said to Adam, "all the misery that you have been made to take upon you because of your transgression, will not free you from the hand of Satan, and will not save you."

XIV: 4

The Lord said, "But I will. When I shall come down from heaven and shall become flesh of thy seed, and take upon Me the infirmity from which you suffer. The darkness that came upon you in this cave shall come upon me in the grave, when I am in the flesh of thy seed."

XIV: 5

"And I, who am without years, shall be subject to the reckoning of years, of times, of months, and of days. And I shall reckon as one of the sons of men, in order to save you."

From Adam an Eve's sin we were all placed in bondage. Subjected to Satan, pain, misery and darkness, meaning the knowledge of God and to commune with God was far away. When a person died they went back to dust into the ground. There was no resurrection back then.

Jesus promise started way back to Adam's days. He stated He was coming back to save and free not only him but who so ever believed in Him, and that He is the Son of the Father our Most High God. He came down to earth to be subjected to Satan's temptations, to be ridiculed with pain, to take away all the sins of the earth.

Everybody's sin was paid for by Jesus, He paid the ultimate debt. He died for you and me, so that we can have everlasting life. No matter what we have done or doing, if we confess our sins, He will throw them away never to be remembered.

That does not mean we can continue to sin. When you receive the Holy Ghost in your life, you will develop a conscience.

Because Jesus came down and saved us, we were set free from bondage. He took us out of darkness into the marvelous light. He made us joint heirs.

He gave us power and authority in His name over Satan.

Now we can see beyond the flesh.

Now we can make the connection of what we say out of our mouth is what will come too past because we have the authority to do so. We must watch what words we speak out our mouth. Our mouth can determine our destiny. God wants us to speak positive and mean what we say. Not begrudging others or have a jealous and unforgiving heart.

Therefore when you get sick, say and mean it, "I am well, and what you say will come to past.

God wants us to have a personal relationship with Him. In order to do so we must read the word, have faith in Him and talk to Him.

We must talk to Him daily, either through pray or just talking naturally to Him to get His advice on the many things happening on earth to us.

The closer we get to Him the less stress we have. We put all our worries in His hand.
Things that use to frighten us before, we won't fear them anymore. We have the right to ask Him for things. We can call ourselves His children, joint heirs to everything.

O how precious the name of Jesus is. His name is Powerful and Holy. He's King of King and Lord of Lord. Yet He died for us.

So please remember who died for you. Who set you free and saved you, So that you can have peace forever more and go back to the Garden of Eden.

Bible Study # 45
From the teaching of Dr. Charles Stanley
Input by Anita Cameron
Bible New International version (NIV)

"In A Father's Footsteps"

Ask yourself the question, if your children walk in your footsteps, will your children walk in the way of the Lord early in their life?

2nd King 21: 19
Amon King of Judah, was twenty-two years old when he became king, and reigned in Jerusalem two years. His mother's name was Meshullemeth daughter of Haruz; she was from Jotbah.

2nd King 21: 20
Amon did evil in the eyes of the Lord, as his father Manasseh had done.

2nd king 21: 21
He walked in all the ways of his father: He worshipped the idols his father had worshipped, and bowed down to them.

2nd King 21: 22
He forsook the Lord, the God of his fathers, and did not walk in the way of the Lord.

How will your children view you?

You set the path of their way.

If your children walk in your way

1. What will they do if they follow your path?
2. Will their life of faith focus on God for their needs?

3. Will they be industrious and set Godly goals for their life?
   a. Do they see you go to work and take care of your family?

   You ask yourself, am I living the kind of life where my children will walk and live in the right path.

   Children make up their mind by what they have been exposed to.

4. Will they be good stewards of their finances or will they find themselves deeply in debt at an early age.

   You do not want to give a child everything they want because that is a Satan notion, so that the child can get out in the world and always be in trouble.

5. Do you teach your child to pray?
   a. Will they make prayer a priority in their life?
   b. How can you teach them to pray? Get on your knees with your children and say lets talk to God together. Or get around the table and say lets talk to God.

6. Will they have a desire to have an intimate relationship with Him?
7. Will they seek to lead other people to Christ?

   If you build character in your children, they will focus on God. Will they do the right thing or the wrong thing? One thing for sure they will think about what is right and what is wrong.

8. Will they faithfully serve the Lord in their local Church?
9. Will they recognize that their body is a Holy Temple of God?
   a. Do they know not to destroy their body and brain with cigarettes, alcohol and drugs?

10. Will they live and work in the power of the Holy Spirit?
11. When they die will they go to heaven?

    Fathers should go to a child and say, "I am saved by the grace of God."

    Fathers should also forgive, as the Lord has forgiven them.

Table of Contents

1. That all may know Him 181
2. The Mystery of Confession 184
3. Patience of God 186
4. Spiritual Warfare 189
5. Spend time with the Holy Spirit 192
6. Letting God handle your burden 194
7. Reality of Redemption 198
8. Confidence: and anointing connector 203
9. What Amazing facts say about Satan 206
10. Guarding your thinking 213
11. The message of the cross 215
12. Living in the power of the Holy Spirit 219
13. The desires of your heart 223
14. Destruction of the Earth 228
15. If you do you are a child of God 232

Bible Study # 46
From the teaching of Charles Stanley
Input by Anita Cameron
Bible—New International Version NIV)

That All May Know Him

The responsibility of every single Christian is to get the gospel to the whole world.

We are to fulfill His desires to get the gospel to the entire world.

1st John 2: 1
My dear children I write this to you so that you will not sin. But if anybody does sin, we have one who speaks to the father in our defense— Jesus Christ, the Righteous One.

1st John 2: 2
He is atoning sacrifice for our sins, and not only for ours but also the sins of the whole world.

1st John 2: 3
We know that we have come to know Him if we obey His commands.

1st John 2: 4
The man that says "I know Him," but does not do what He commands is a liar, and the truth is not in him.

1st John 2: 5
But if anyone obeys His word, God's love is truly made complete in him. This is how we know we are in Him.

1st John 2: 6
Whosoever claims to live in Him must walk as Jesus did.

1ˢᵗ John 2: 7
Dear friend I am not writing you a new command but an old one, which you have had since the beginning. This old command is the message you have heard.

1ˢᵗ John 2: 8
Yet I am not writing you a new command; its truth is seen in Him and you, because the darkness is passing and the true light is already shinning.

1ˢᵗ John 2: 9
Anyone who claims to be in the light but hates his brother is still in the darkness.

He cleansed us from all our sins.

He has a desire that we know Him and be saved.

What Motivates God

1. He understands our motivation to do sin.
2. His love for us.

Romans 5: 5
And hope does not disappoint us, because God has poured out His love into our hearts by the Holy Spirit, whom He has given us.

*Romans **5: 6***
You see, at just the right time, when we were still powerless, Christ died for the ungodly.

Romans 5: 7
Very rarely will anyone die for a righteous man, though for a good man someone might possibly dare to die.

Romans 5: 8
But God demonstrates His own love for us in this: While we were still sinners, Christ died for us.

3. God's plan for our life.

> On judgment day when we stand up before Him, He is not going to bring up our sins. He is going to reward us.

> Everything your heart desires, Jesus provides for you.

> We have a testimony, and we impact people around us.

> The Holy Spirit comes into your life and you become a new creature.

JEHOVAH GOD DESIRES THAT THE WHOLE WORLD BE SAVED THROUGH HIS SON JESUS.

Bible Study # 47
From the teaching of Pastor Bill Winston
Input also made by Anita Cameron.
Bible, New International version (NIV)

The Mystery of Confession

What comes out of your mouth will affect your life.

What's in your heart will come out your mouth.

It's more than noise, its spirit.

Hidden Truth

The truth has been hidden. What you speak is what you will receive. The Earth is governed by words. This is a word Planet.

Therefore we all have to watch what we say.

We must clean up our speech and speak right words.

Cleanse your heart, and make sure the right stuff comes out of your mouth.

The Tower of Babel

Genesis 11: 1-9
Now the whole world had one language and a common speech. As men moved eastward, they found a plain in Shinar and settled there.

They said to each other, "Come, let's make bricks and bake them thoroughly." They used brick instead of stone, and tar for mortar. Then they said, "Come let us build ourselves a city, with a tower that reaches to the heavens, so that we may make a name for ourselves and not be scattered over the face of the whole earth."

But the Lord came down to see the city and the tower that the men were building. The Lord said," if as one people speaking the same language they have begun to do this, then nothing they plan to do will be impossible for them. Come, let us go down and confuse their language so they will not understand each other."

So the Lord scattered them from there over all the earth, and they stopped building the city.

That is why it is called Babel, because there the Lord confused the language of the whole world. From there the Lord scattered them over the face of the whole earth.

Numbers 14:2
Just like when the Israelites grumbled against Moses and Aaron, and the whole assembly said to them, "If only we had died in Egypt! Or in this desert!

They received their request. What came out of there mouth happened. They stayed in the desert for 40 years and that generation died there. Then the Lord gave the generation after the promise land, filled with milk and honey.

You are not going to see anything in your life any different then what comes out of your mouth.

God has established that no one can determine your future but you. No principalities, no system, can govern your life.

Whatever you have in your heart in abundance will come out of your mouth.

Any man and woman in Christ is a new creature.
And the devil is a liar.

You are going to get your inheritance. The problem is your mouth and your tongue.

If you put your words on it, there is nothing people can do to stop you.

Remember the fear of the Lord is wisdom; and to depart from evil is understanding.

Bible Study # 48
From the teachings of Dr. Charles Stanley
Input by Anita Cameron
Bible: King James Version (KJV)
New International Version(NIV)

Patience Of God

God is slothful to anger, meaning slow to anger.

Are you on thin ice with God?

2nd Peter 3: 3
Knowing this first, that there shall come in the last day scoffer (men and women), walking after their own lusts.

2nd Peter 3:4
And they will be saying, "Where is the promise of His coming? For since the fathers fell asleep (meaning died) all things continue as they were from the beginning of the creation."

2nd Peter 3:5
For this they (the scoffers) are willingly ignorant of, that by the word of God the heavens were of old, and the earth standing out of the water and in the water.

2nd Peter 3:6
Where by the world that then was, being overflowed with water perished.

2nd Peter 3: 7
But the heavens and the earth which are now, by the same word are kept in store, reserved unto fire against the Day of Judgment and perdition of ungodly men.

2nd Peter 3: 8
But beloved, be not ignorant of this one thing, that one day is with the Lord as a thousand years, and a thousand years as one day.

2nd Peter 3: 9
The Lord is not slack concerning His promise, as some men count slackness, but is long suffering towards us; not willing that any should perish, but that all should come to repentance.

When we sin, we are choosing to be rebellious against God.

People think God is overlooking it because they continue to sin and nothing is happening to them, in fact they think they are doing great.

Guess what, often times its already happening to them. It started, and before long they will see that the wages of sin is death and that they cannot get away with it.

God does not over look sin.

He gives the unsaved time to be saved

Look at Adam and Eve; there was an immediate consequence to their sin. They were evicted out of the Garden of Eden to fend for themselves.

When people start abusing drugs and alcohol and stealing, it's just a matter of time before they become addicted to what they are doing. By the time they realize they are destroying their life they are already hooked.

1st Timothy 1: 12
I thank Christ Jesus our Lord, who has given me strength, that He considered me faithful, appointing me to His service.

1st Timothy 1: 13
Even though I was once a blasphemer and a persecutor and a violent man, I was shown mercy because I acted in ignorance and unbelief.

1st Timothy 1: 14
The grace of our Lord was poured out on me abundantly, along with the faith and love that are in Christ Jesus.

1st Timothy 1: 15
Here is a trustworthy saying that deserves full acceptance: Christ Jesus came into the world to save sinners—of whom I am the worst.

1ˢᵗ Timothy 1: 16
But for that very reason I was shown mercy so that in me, His unlimited patience as an example for those who would believe on Him and receive eternal life.

If you continue to sin you are storing up sin for the wrath of God.

Why God is Patience

1. He's giving people the opportunity to get saved.

   Those people, who don't believe in God, He is going to show up in their life anyway and that is going to shock them.

2. Ignorance of God's word.

   He knows we came into this world with an innate nature away from God.

   All of us have an area of weakness in our life.

   We have this tendency to live worldly.

   It is time for us to listen. It's time for Him to get the gospel to us.

   It's time for people to stand up, worship, live a godly life and confess their faith to others

2ⁿᵈ Peter 3: 10
But the day of the Lord will come like a thief in the night. The heavens will disappear with a roar; the element will be destroyed by fire, and the earth and everything in it will be laid bare.

Bible Study # 49
From the teaching of Dr. Bill Winston.
Input also by Anita Cameron
Bible: King James Version (KJV)

Spiritual Warfare

There's more in the unseen ream than in the seen.

Ephesians 6:12
For we wrestle not against flesh and blood, but against principalities, against powers, against the rulers of the darkness of this world, against spiritual wickedness in high places.

There is demonic control.

We are on an assignment here. The Church is the responsible agent for holding back iniquities. We are holding back Satan from taken over.

The devil couldn't stop you from being saved, but he's trying to stop you from being effective.

Satan is going to try to use all the power he has to prevent you from being effective.

Satan doesn't have more power than Jesus.

We have a distorted thinking about Satan. In the movies they try to scare people by illustrating Satan as having power over the earth.

Satan has no power. The only power he has is what we let him have.

When Jesus came to the earth in the flesh and died for our sins, all power was given to Him over the heavens and the earth.

You can't fight Satan, he and is disciples have already been defeated.

When Satan comes up against you, he's really coming up against God. Because there's a job you were sent to do and Jesus has dedicated you to do the job.

Jesus has given us authority and power. We are supposed to cast the devil out of people.

How are we going to cast out the devil?

How are we going to hold back iniquities?

1. Everyday we must pray.
2. Everyday we must get into the Bible.
3. You must have faith.

Faith comes by hearing, and hearing by the word of God.

Jesus is seated far above on the right hand side of the Father.

Ephesians 2:6
And He has raised us up together, and made us sit together in heavenly places in Christ Jesus.

We represent the whole armor of God. We are to hold back iniquities.

Jesus is our advocator, He is our lawyer, who has never lost a case.

Ephesians 6:13
Wherefore take unto you the whole armor of God that you may be able to withstand in the evil day and having done all to stand.

Ephesians 6: 14
Stand therefore, having your lions girt about with truth, and having on the breastplate of righteousness.

Ephesians 6: 15
And your feet shod with the preparation of the gospel of peace.

Ephesians 6: 16
Above all, taking the shield of faith, wherewith you shall be able to quench all the fiery darts of the wicked.

Ephesians 6: 17
And "take the helmet of salvation, and the sword of the Spirit, which is the word of God.

Ephesians 6:18
Praying always with all prayer and supplication in the Spirit, and watching there with all perseverance and supplication for all saints.

Bible Study # 50
From the teaching Dr. Dollar
Input also by Anita Cameron
Bible: King James Version (KJV)

Spend Time With The Holy Spirit

He is our unseen partner.

He empowers us, guides us, counsel us, teaches us, comforts us, reveals things to us, and bring things to our memory.

God knows the thoughts and plans for my life and your life.

Jeremiah 29: 11
For I know the thoughts that I think toward you, said the Lord, thoughts of peace, and not of evil, to give you and expected end.

To give you hope in your final outcome is peace, welfare not evil things, because God has nothing evil for you.

Whenever you stop fooling around in the flesh and get with God, you will see that our final is better than our present situation, therefore you cannot quit.

Ephesians 3: 3
Paul states how by revelations Jesus made known to him the mystery!

Ephesians 3:5
Which in others ages was not made known unto the sons of men, as it is now revealed unto His holy apostles and prophets by the Spirit;

Ephesians 3: 9
To make all men see what is the fellowship of the mystery, which from the beginning of the world has been hid in God, who created all things by Jesus Christ.

Revelation is revealed knowledge.

It is revealed by the Holy Spirit. Without the Holy Spirit you will not get exact knowledge.

Ephesians 2: 10
For we are His workmanship created in Christ Jesus unto good works, which God has before ordained that we should walk in them.

We have a personal tutor. When you open the Bible the Holy Spirit will help you understand. He is the author of the Bible.

He told all the prophets and saints what to write in the Bible.

The Holy Spirit is your enlightenment to show you your path.

Everyday talk to the Holy Spirit, Spend time fellowshipping with Him, and eventually you will know His voice. He is the one who will lead you away from trouble into glory.

Bible Study # 51
From the Teaching of Dr. Charles Stanley,
Input also by Anita Cameron,
From the Bible: King James version(KJV)
And the New Believers Bible (NBB).

Letting God Handle Your Burdens

Psalm 38:4
For mine iniquities are gone over mind head: As a heavy burden they are too heavy for me.

We forget how blessed we are that we don't have to bare our burdens alone.

Matthew 11:28
Jesus said, "Come unto me all you that labor and are heavy laden, and I will give you rest.

Matthew 1:29
Take my yoke upon you, and learn of me; for I am meek and lowly in heart, and you shall find rest unto your souls".

Matthew 11:30
For my yoke is easy and my burden is light."

New Believers Bible 11:28
Jesus said, "come to me, all of you who are weary and carry heavy burdens, and I will give you rest.

NBB 11:29
Take my yoke upon you, let me teach you, because I am humble and gentle, and you will find rest for your souls.

NBB 11:30
For my yoke fits perfectly, and the burden I give you is light.

What motivates Jesus our Lord and Savior to handle our burdens?

1. Because people are burden with sin.

    Living with sin is a horrible burden to carry.

    If you don't have Jesus in your life, you will never know peace.

2. Jesus is motivated by love.

    God is full of love for us and He does not want us to live in bondage.

3. Being burden down because of what people have done to you and said about you.

    Jesus loves you no matter who you are.

Psalm 55:22
Cast your burden upon the Lord, and He shall sustain you: He shall never suffer the righteous to be moved.

NBB 55:22
Give your burdens to the Lord and He will take care of you. He will not permit the godly to slip and fall.

Our Lord God will motivate you and equip you because we all have different burdens. For example:

a. Some people have financial burdens.
b. Some people have relationship burdens.
c. Some people have Children burdens.
d. Some people have sin burdens.

Psalm 68:19
Bless the Lord, who daily loaded us with benefits, even the God of our salvation.

NBB 68:19
Praise the Lord; praise God our savior! For each day He carries us in His arms.

Whatever burdens you have God will make you able to live in the mist of it and talk it out.

Burdens cause anxiety and worry. God does not want us to have anxiety and He most certainly does not want us to worry about anything.

The Lord is handling it. I don't have to worry about it.

Surrender yourself to the will of God, because our master has all good things and love for us. He will take the weight off us.

If you don't trust Him, He will not do it.

Proverbs 3: 5
Trust the Lord with all your heart; and lean not unto your own understanding.

Proverbs 3:6
In all your ways acknowledge Him, and He shall direct your path.

He will not only direct your path, but He will show you your path.

Watch and see how He deals in your life.

Jesus knows what is going on in our lives because of what He is, because of what He said, and because He has all power.

God is Omnipotence (all Power)
God is Omnipresent (Everywhere at all times)
God is Omniscience (Knowing everything)

He knows all things, past, present and future. Nothing goes beyond His knowledge.

God knows every circumstance.

It's time for you to surrender yourself to the Lord and trust Him.

You don't have to fast and plead or make promises to God.

If you are a believer you don't have to take on your burdens.

Oh God if they just knew who you are.

Bible Study # 52
From the teachings of Pastor Bill Winston
Input also by Anita Cameron
From the King James Version of the bible(KJV),
And the New Believers Bible,(NBB)

Reality of Redemption

Jesus paid for our redemption.

He set us free from bondage.

Christianity is not about pain, suffering and struggle.

Matthew 10: 28
And fear not them which can kill body, but which is able to destroy both soul and body in hell.

Matthew 10: 29
Are not two sparrows sold for a farthing (half a penny)?
And not one of them will fall on the ground without your Father.

Matthew 10:30
But the hairs of your head are all numbered.

Matthew 10: 31
Fear not therefore, you are more valuable than many sparrows.

Religion has the idea that, I'm suffering in the Lord, and that's wrong.
Christ suffered for us.

1st Peter 4: 12
Beloved think it not strange concerning the trial which is to try you, as though some strange thing happened unto you.

*1ˢᵗ **Peter** 4: 13*
But rejoice, in as much you are partakers of Christ suffering: that, when His glory shall be revealed you may be glad also with exceeding joy.

We are partakers, meaning take up your part in Christ suffering.

Christ became sin on the cross.

When He died, we became righteous.

He was wounded, so that we can be healed.

He became poor so that we can become rich.

My part is not getting sick.

My part is to stay healthy.

My Jesus suffered so that I can be free.

Matthew 6: 9
And lead us not into temptation (tested or tried).

Heaven is full of joy and happiness and God wants the same for the earth.

A lot of God's inheritance has not been received of His people, because they feel they are not worthy.

Wait until you go to heaven. The streets are made of gold and the houses are mansions.

Jesus was rich and He became poor so that you can become rich.

He wants us to be rich in spirit, money, knowledge, wisdom, kindness, and love and in all things.

If you have rejections of being rich then you don't believe God's word.

We have to renew our mind. We are our greatest let down; because we feel we are not worthy.

Part of our redemption is when we ask forgiveness for our sins and mean it.

Isaiah 44: 22
Jesus said, "I have blotted out, as a thick cloud, thy transgressions, and, as a cloud, thy sins: Return unto me; for I have redeemed thee.

Then all our sins are remembered no more.

Of course watch out for Satan, he will try to constantly bring them to your memory. Pay no attention to him, because The Lord has removed our transgressions from us.

Jesus came into the earth to redeem us. It is time for us to take back what belongs to us.

If the devil (Satan) knew what he was doing, he never would have crucified Him.

When Jesus was crucified we were redeemed.

Remember Jesus submitted Himself to death, they didn't kill Him.

They strike and bruised His Spirit.

He was beaten, beaten and beaten, to take us into the spirit, so that we can be spiritual minded.

To be carnal minded is death.

To be spiritual minded is peace.

Jesus had so much life flowing in Him, that when He walked in the room everyone felts His presents.

He submitted Himself to death, they didn't kill Him, so, when He gave up the ghost, He kept the old covenant law perfect. You are in Him, and you must keep it perfect.

When Jesus said "My God, My God, why have you forsaken me, He became sin, who knew no sin. He took on the sins of the whole world.

Jesus had become iniquity. He had no clothes on, and being naked was a disgrace.

When He died Satan ushered Him down to hell. He who was incorruptible became corruptible to save and free us from bondage.

On the third day Jesus was resurrected.

Luke 24: 7
Jesus said, "The Son of man must be delivered into the hands of sinful men, and be crucified, and the third day rise again.

Luke 24: 27
Jesus said, "Beginning at Moses and all the prophets, He expounded unto them in all the scriptures the things concerning Himself."

NBB **Luke 24: 46**
Jesus said unto the Apostles, "Yes it was written long ago that the Messiah must suffer and die and rise again from the dead on the third day.

NBB Luke 24: 47
Jesus said, "With my authority, take this message of repentance to all the nations, beginning in Jerusalem: There is forgiveness of sins for all who turn to me.

Look how blessed we are. The blood of Jesus redeemed us.

That's why when you are in the Lord and die; the Angels come for you, because you have been purchased by the blood of Jesus. And while on earth you are protected.

Psalm 91:9
Because thou have made the Lord, which is my refuge, even the most high, thou habitation;

Psalm 91: 10
There shall no evil befall thee, neither shall any plague come near thy dwelling.

Psalm 91: 11
For He shall give His Angels charge over thee, to keep thee in all thy ways.

Psalm 91: 14
Jesus said, "Because he has set His love upon me, therefore I will deliver him; I will set him on high, because he have known my name.

Psalm 91:15
He shall call upon me, and I will answer him: I will be with him in trouble; I will deliver him, and honor him.

Psalm 91: 16
With long life will I satisfy him and show him my salvation.

NBB Psalm 91: 14-16
The Lord says, "I will rescue those who love me.
I will protect those who trust in my name.

Psalm 91: 15
When they call on me, I will answer: I will be with them in trouble.
I will rescue them and honor them.

Psalm 91: 16
I will satisfy them with a long life and give them my salvation.

Bible Study # 53
From the teaching of Dr Creflo Dollar
Input also by Anita Cameron
Bible: King James Version (KJV) and
The living Bible (TLB)

Confidence:
and Anointing Connector

Knowledge that comes from God to you, gives you confidence.

When you say I am blessed, your whole body hears and feels that you are blessed.

What the enemy attacks is your confidence.

Satan loves to attack your confidence because it lessens your trust in God.

We have to be careful not to let Satan attack our confidence.

Our confidence is God's word and what He promises.

KJV Isaiah 30: 15
For thus said the Lord, the Holy one of Israel; In returning and rest shall you be saved; In quietness and in confidence shall be your strength: and you would not.

TLB Isaiah 30: 15
For the Lord God, the Holy One of Israel say, only in returning to me waiting for me will you be saved; in quietness and confidence is your strength, but you'll have none of this.

In order to attack my confidence, Satan attacks my strength.

KJV 1ˢᵗ John 3: 20
For if my heart condemn us, God is greater than heart, and knows all things.

KJV 1ˢᵗ John 3: 21
Beloved if our heart condemn us not then have we confidence toward God.

If the enemy is going to mess with my condemnation—my feeling of I am not doing enough. I am not praying enough etc.

Condemnation destroys strength

Say, "I will not allow condemnation in my life.

I will have assurance of the mind—a firm belief, trust, and reliance—relying on God who is love.

Faith is a practical expression of your confidence and God and His word.

It is going to be Trust, Faith and Confidence.

What I see won't move me.

I've got to move with what I know, and I know that God loves me.

He's JEHOVAH—JIREH—MY provider.

He's JEHOVAH—NISSE—He fights my battles when I am right.

He's JEHOVAH—SHALOM—He gives me peace.

He's JEHOVAH—ROPHE—He heals me.

He's JEHOVAH—TSIDKENU—He's my righteousness.

He's JEHOVAH—SHAMMAH—He's always present with me.

He's JEHOVAH—ROHI—He's my Good Shepherd. He is always watching over me.

KJV Isaiah 26: 4
Lord Jehovah is everlasting strength.

I trust God and I will not be moved.

KJV Proverbs 3: 5
Trust in the Lord with all your heart; and lean not unto your own understanding.

KJV Proverbs 3: 6
In all your ways acknowledge Him, and He shall direct your paths.

The Glory is about to hit your glory.

The manifestation of God is about to hit your house.

Now is the time to find your footing.

Whatever the devil to trying to bring to you, you are holding that trust in God.

I know a God that can change all things. You've got to trust in Him.

Know matter how messy your life is, He loves you.

Bible Study # 54
From the teachings of Doug Bachelor
Input by Anita Cameron
Bible King James Bible (KJB),
New Believers Bible (NBB)
And the teaching from Pastor Noel Jones

What amazing facts do the Bible reveals regarding Satan's method to hurt, deceive, discourage and destroy people?

Satan, also known as the Devil, was once an angel in heaven named Lucifer.

He was an exalted angel, but he tried to up seat God, His creator, and demanded that all would worship him.

And there was a war in heaven between Michael and his angels, and Satan and his angels. One third of the angels in heaven joined Satan.

Satan did not prevail, he was defeated and cast out of heaven down to earth.

Lucifer was created by God, as were all the other Angels.

Ezekiel 28: 13
God said to Lucifer, "You were in Eden, the garden of God. Your clothing was adorned with every precious stone. Red carnelian, chrysolite, white moonstone, beryl, onyx, jasper, sapphire, turquoise, and emerald. All beautifully crafted for you and set in the finest gold. They were given to you on the day you were created."

Ezekiel 28: 14
God said, "I ordained and anointed you as the mighty angelic guardian. You had access to the holy mountain of God and walked among the stones of fire."

Ezekiel 28: 15
God said, "You were blameless in all you did from the day you were created until the day evil was found in you.

Ezekiel 28: 16
God said, "Your great wealth filled you with violence, and you sinned. So I banished you from the mountain of God. I expelled you, O mighty guardian, from your place among the stones of fire."

Ezekiel 28: 17
God said, "Your heart was filled with pride because of all your beauty. You corrupted your wisdom for the sake of your splendor. So I threw you to the earth and exposed you to the curious gaze of kings.

Lucifer's discontent became open rebellion against God. One-third of heaven angels joined him in an attempt to overthrow God. As a result, Lucifer and his followers were cast out of heaven.

Lucifer was called Satan (adversary) and devil (slanderer), and his angels were called demons.

Satan uses every conceivable way to deceive and destroy people. His demons can appear and pose as righteous people, even clergyman. And Satan will appear as a glorious angel of light and power to call fire down from heaven. He will impersonate Jesus. But you have now been warned, so don't fall for it.

When Jesus comes back every eye will see Him.

Revelation 1:7
Look! He (Jesus) comes with the clouds of heaven. And everyone will see Him. Even those who pierce Him and all the nations of the earth will weep because of Him. Yes! AMEN

Jesus will remain in the cloud and not even touch earth.

1ˢᵗ *Thessalonians 4: 17*
Then, together with Him, we who are still alive and remain on the earth will be caught up in the clouds to meet the Lord in the air and remain with Him forever.

So don't fall for the deception that will be displayed by Satan.

Satan deceives and persecutes

Revelations 12: 9
This great dragon, the ancient serpent called the Devil, or Satan, the one deceiving the whole world, was thrown down to the earth with all his angels.

Revelations 12: 13
And when the dragon realized that he had been thrown down to the earth, he pursued the woman who had given birth to the child.

Satan falsely accuses/murders

Revelations 12: 10
Then I heard a loud voice shouting across the heavens. "It has happened at last, the salvation and power and kingdom of our God, and the authority of His Christ! For the accuser has been thrown down to earth, the one who accused our brothers and sisters before our God day and night.

John 8:44
For you are the children of your father the devil, and you love to do the evil things he does. He was a murderer from the beginning and has always hated the truth. There is no truth in him. When he lies, it is consistent with his character, for he is a liar, and the father of lies.

Satan makes war against God's people

Revelations 12:17
Then the dragon (Satan) became angry at the woman, and he declared war against the rest of her children, and all who keep God's commandments and confess that they belong to Jesus.

Satan quotes an misquotes the Bible—he even tried to tempt Jesus.

Matthew 4: 5-6
Then the Devil took Jesus to Jerusalem to the highest point of the temple, and said, "If you are the Son of God, jump off! For the scriptures say, "He orders His Angels to protect you, and they will hold you with their hands to keep you from striking your foot on a stone."

Matthew 4: 7
Jesus told him, "The Scriptures also say, do not test the Lord your God."

Satan works miracles and lies.

Revelation 16: 13
And I saw three evil spirits that looked like frogs leap from the mouth of the dragon, the beast, and the false prophets.

Revelations 16: 14
These miracles—working demons caused all the rulers of the world to gather for battle against the Lord on that great judgment day of God Almighty.

Satan brings disease and affliction.

Job 2:7
So Satan left the Lord's presence, and he struck job with a terrible case of boils from head to foot.

Satan appears as angel of light and his demons impersonates pastors.

2nd Corinthians 11: 13
These people are false apostles. They have fooled you by disguising themselves as apostles of Christ.

2nd Corinthians 11: 14
But I am not surprised! Even Satan can disguise himself as an angel of light.

2nd Corinthians 11: 15
So it is no wonder his servants can also do it by pretending to be godly ministers. In the end they will get every bit of punishment their wicked deeds deserve.

Satan's present headquarters

There's no place for Satan in heaven after he was cast out.

Satan's headquarters is in the earth, not hell.

God gave Adam and Eve dominion over the earth. When they sinned, they lost it to Satan, who then became ruler, or prince of the earth.

Satan bitterly hates humans, who were created in God's image.

He can't touch God so instead; he directed his viciousness against people who are God's children.

He's a hateful, vicious murderer whose aim is to destroy you and thus hurt God.

He cannot destroy you unless you let him.

To make the final complete eradication of sin from the universe, God sent His only begotten Son to earth to take back the authority that Satan took from Adam and Eve, and gave it back to us, the children of God.

KJV 1ˢᵗ John 3: 8
He that committed sin is of the Devil. For the Devil sinned from the beginning. "For this purpose The Son of God was manifested, that He might destroy the works of the Devil.

Hebrew 2:14
Because God's children are human beings, made of flesh and blood, Jesus also became flesh and blood by being born in human form. For only as a human being could He die and only dying could He break the power of the Devil, who had the power of death.

Hebrew 2: 17
Therefore it was necessary for Jesus to be in every respect like us, His brothers and sisters, so that He could be our merciful and faithful priest before God. He then could offer a sacrifice that would take away the sins of the people.

Hebrew 2:18
Since He Himself has gone through suffering and temptation, He is able to help us when we are being tempted.

Pastor Noel Jones said "Jesus said, I saw Satan dropped like lighting from the sky."

The devil will tell you all kinds of lies. He never tells the truth.

He has a way of fooling people, even children of God.

That's why you have to read your Bible to stay fast in your faith.

Satan comes to kill and destroy, he watches you and tries to find ways to destroy you. He tries to learn your weaknesses so that he can constantly tempt you.

The Devil knows how to move on you. He disguises himself as though he's a saint, but inside he is all evil.

The devil has his own church, His own demons and he employs false teachers.

God has given my Spirit to me. I will not let Satan destroy me.

We have news for the Devil. We have a breastplate of righteousness, and a Helmet of salvation.

Remember out of your heart is what you speak. Watch how you think.

Now you realize you have the power to stand and resist and rebuke Satan, because God has you covered.

Say this prayer

God thank you for giving me your word, your love and strength to rebuke Satan and to recognize him for who he is.

Thank you God for pulling the covers off some of my friends to let me know where they are and that they mean me no good. AMEN

Remember, sometimes you have to remove yourself from certain situations and people, because they are continually dealing with the Devil.

Also remember that Satan can only suggest things to you, don't fall for it.

Bible Study # 55
From the teaching of Dr. Creflo Dollar
Input by Anita Cameron
KJV Bile and NBB Bible

"Guarding Your Thinking"

Acts of perversion is Satan who disrupts your thinking and causes your emotions to take control over your life.

Your emotions should not control your life.

If Satan can get his disruption in the Garden of Eden, then, if he could he would have darkness all over the world.

Had Eve had a second thought, she might not have followed the serpent's suggestion.

The most power of Satan is suggestion. He'll say something to get you to have second thoughts.

Second thoughts: about your salvation, your calling, and about the word.

He does that in order to move you out of the will of God.

Words will determine your thinking.
Your thinking will determine your emotions.
And your emotion will determine your decisions.

Everything starts with words: In the Kingdom of God and in the world.

John 1: 1
In the beginning was the Word, and the Word was with God, and the Word was God.

John 1: 2
The same was in the beginning with God.

Satan wants you to think opposing to the word of God.

God asked Adam in Genesis 3: 11

Who told you that you were naked?

In other words, who have been framing your way of thinking?

That's why sometimes you have to get away from friends and family, that are trying to frame your way of thinking from God's will.

Instead of letting your emotions rule your life, you must let the Word of God rule your life.

When you allow emotions to take over your life, you become perverted.

You will allow jealousy, selfishness, and feeling insecure and unloved take over your life.

Once that happens you become occupied with emotions and your decision making becomes obscured.

There are good emotions and there are bad emotions.

Good emotions are easy to determine.

You are happy that your child is graduating from school, etc.

You have waited on the Lord for something and it is here.

Guard your thinking by reading the word of God, and keeping it in your heart and mind.

Learn how to take over your emotions.

Bible Study # 56
From the teachings of Dr. Charles Stanley
Input also by Anita Cameron
Bible: King James Version(KJV)
And The New Believers Bible(NBB)

The Message of The Cross

Why do people wear a cross?

What is the message you're sending when you wear a cross?

Most Christians cannot tell you the message of the cross.

Galatians 6:14
Apostle Paul said, "As for me, God forbid that I should boast about anything except the cross of our Lord Jesus Christ. Because of that cross, my interest in this world died long ago, and the world's interest in me is also long dead."

1st Corinthians 1: 17
Paul said, "For Christ didn't send me to baptize, but to preach the good news and not with clever speeches and high sounding ideas, for fear that the cross of Christ would lose its powers.

The cross is more than something you wear or sing about.

1st Corinthians 1:18
I knew very well how foolish the message of the cross sounds to those who are on the road to destruction. But we who are being saved recognize this message as the very power of God.

1st Corinthians 1: 19
As the Scriptures say: "I will destroy human wisdom and discard their most brilliant ideas."

1ˢᵗ Corinthians 1; 20
So where does this leave the philosophers, the scholars, and the world's brilliant debaters? God has made them all look foolish and has shown their wisdom to be useless nonsense.

1ˢᵗ Corinthians 1: 21
Since god in His wisdom saw to it that the world would never find Him through wisdom, He has used our foolish preaching to save all who believe.

1ˢᵗ Corinthians 1: 22
God's way seems foolish to the Jews because they want a sign from heaven to prove it is true. And it is foolish to the Greeks because they believe only what agrees with their wisdom.

1ˢᵗ Corinthians 1:23
So when we preach that Christ was crucified, the Jews are offended, and the Gentiles say it's all nonsense.

1ˢᵗ Corinthians 1: 24
But to those called by God to salvation, both Jews and Gentiles, Christ is the mighty power of God and the wonderful wisdom of God.

1srt Corinthians 1:25
This "foolish" plan of God is far wiser than the wisest of human plans, and God's weakness is far stronger than the greatest of human strength.

What is the Cross about?

The first is the expression of the justice of God

Justice—God is right and always does the right thing. He's faith and always faith.

All of us are under the judgment of God.

God hates sin.

You can excuse it and deny it, but God hates sin. Adultery, murder, stealing, idol worshipping or any other form of sin, God hates sin.

The justice of God must be answered, because we are all guilty of sin.

Every single religion in the world thinks they have to do something to please God.

What God did to deal with our sins, He made a choice.

The cross—He sent His Son Jesus, the only sinless person in the world, to die for all the sins of the world since Adam.

In order for God to accept us He sent His Son to the cross.

Now God can forgive us for our sins.

He sent His Son in our place.

That's God's Justice.

The cross is not about love, it's about the justice of God to put in a substitute for us.

It can't be for your good works.

God does not deal with your works.

He looks at the change on the inside of you.

When you accept Jesus, then you are changed inside.

So the cross is about God's Justice.

The second is the Expression of God's Wisdom

Man's way is something that man does.

God does not let man take credit for His works.

God came up with the awesome plan and it is our acceptance by Him through His Son Jesus.

God knew man could not change.

He came to earth to live as a man and pay for our sins.

He did it in such a fashion that He took full responsibility for our sins and for our forgiveness.

The moment a person says I want to receive Lord Jesus as my personal savior, through Jesus and Jesus along they have eternal life.

Thirdly is God's Love

God loves us all, but God's love for us does not let God look over sin.

Except a man be born again, you cannot have eternal life.

You have to be a believer.

I ask Him to forgive me of my sins because He paid the price.

It doesn't mean I can sin and get away with it, because God will chastise me if I continue to do the same sin.

You must keep the faith in Jesus Christ, the only begotten Son.

The fourth is the Power of God

It doesn't make a difference who you are and how old you are, it takes the same amount of power to save a 10 year old boy as it is to save a 90 year old man.

The cross is the symbol of the finish work of Jesus for our sins.

It is the power to give us absolute assurance that He has made us free.

The cross is an expression of Justice, wisdom, Love and the Power of God in one event in time.

Hallelujah
(Praise ye JEHOVAH)

Bible Study # 57
From the teaching of Dr Charles Stanley,
Input also by Anita Cameron
Bible: King James Version (KJV) and
New Beginners Bible Version (NNB)

Living In The Power of The Holy Spirit

The Holy Spirit, a personal Helper.

He's living on the inside of us.

If we listen to His guidance we will not stray (take the wrong path).

Most people will not listen, because it is something they don't want to hear.

When they decide to do what they want to do and avoid what the Holy Spirit is telling them, they suffer the consequence of their behavior. They will either blame someone else or blame the situation. But, in their heart they know it was revealed to them in advance.

The Holy Spirit was given to us through the Father and Jesus.

John 14:16
Jesus said, "I will pray the Father, and He shall give you another Comforter.

John 14:26
The Comforter, which is the Holy Spirit, whom the father will send in my name, He shall teach you all things and bring all things to your remembrance, whatsoever I have said to you.

The Holy Spirit is our Helper

He knows about the future. He walks along side of us, to enables us and helps us.

We all need help.

The Holy Spirit is available at all times.

He is Omniscience (knowing everything)

He is Omnipresent (He is inside of us, present at all times)

The Holy Spirit is an adequate Helper.

He is a dependable Helper.

The Holy Spirit was sent to us by God and Jesus, He is very Wise.

One of the reasons you don't have joy inside is because you don't listen.

You cannot be lazy, sloftful and disobedient.

We have no excuse not to live a godly life.

The Holy Spirit helps us in our Pray life.

Sometimes we don't know how to pray, what to pray for, and to kneel to pray.

KJV Romans 8: 26
The Spirit also help our infirmities: for we know not what we should pray for as we ought: but the Spirit itself make intercession for us with groaning which cannot be uttered.

NBB **Romans 8: 26**
And the Holy Spirit helps us in our distress, for we don't even know what we should pray for, or how we should. But the Holy Spirit prays for us with groanings that cannot be expressed in words.

NBB Romans 8: 27
And the Father who knows all hearts knows what the Spirit is saying, for the Spirit pleads for us believers in harmony with God's own will.

KJV Romans 8: 16
The Spirit itself bear witness with our spirit that we are the children of God.

The Holy Spirit keeps me aware of my unworthiness and God's Power and Holiness.

The Holy Spirit helps us understand the word of God

KJV 1st Corinthians 2: 14
But the natural man receives not the things of the Spirit of God: For they are foolishness unto him: Neither can he know them, because they are spiritually discerned.

NBB 1st Corinthians 2:14
But people who aren't Christians can't understand these truths from God's Spirit. It all sounds foolish to them because only those who have the Spirit can understand what the Spirit means.

KJV 1st Corinthians 2: 10
But God has revealed them unto us by His Spirit: For the Spirit search all things, yea, the deep things of God.

NBB 1st Corinthians 2:10
But we know these things because God has revealed them to us by His Spirit, and His Spirit searches out everything and shows us even God's deep secrets.

When you read the word of God, the Spirit of God gives you understanding in the word of God at our point in life.

The Holy Spirit Convicts us of our sin.

Dealing with sin, The Holy Spirit helps in the moments of weakness and frailty.

He knows when your body needs recharging.

The Holy Spirit helps when tempted to doubt The Lord's truth and promises.

Through difficult times of sorrow and heartache The Holy Spirit is there.

Remember you don't bury saints.

Absent from the body, present with The Lord.

The Holy Spirit helps by giving us spiritual gifts for the work God has called us to do.

The Spirit God is not going to fight with you. He's there to equip you.

Do you want peace, joy, love, faithfulness, goodness, self-control, and kindness?

Well you've got it that's the fruit of The Holy Spirit.

If you don't have it, then you have to surrender yourself to The Holy Spirit.

Surrender your life to God, Yield to the Holy Spirit so that you can experience, joy, love and peace and all the above.

You surrender your life totally to The Lord and these characteristics will be in you through the Holy Spirit our helper.

When you lose love, joy, peace understanding, look inside you, and The Holy Spirit will show you why.

The Holy Spirit is God's personal Helper given to us to enable us.

He is for our asking.

Bible Study # 58
From the teaching of Dr. Charles Stanley,
Input also by Anita Cameron,
Bible: King James Version (KJV)

The Desires of Your Heart

God said he would give us the desires of our life, but we must remember our desires are sometimes not good for us. Therefore we must talk and pray to the Lord so that our desires are consistent with His desires for you.

Sometimes you desire something that you feel others have gotten, and why not you.

Psalm 37 1: 1
Don't worry about the wicked. Don't envy those who do wrong.

Psalm 37 1: 2
For like grass they soon fade away. Like springtime flowers, they wither.

Psalm 37 1: 3
Trust in the Lord and do good. Then you will live safely in the land and prosper.

Psalm 37 1: 4
Take delight in the Lord, and He will give you your heart's desires.

Psalm 37 1: 5
Commit everything you do to the Lord. Trust Him and He will help you.

Psalm 37 1: 6
He will make your innocence as clear as the dawn, and the justice of your cause will shine like the noonday sun.

Psalm 37 1: 7
Be Still in the presence of the Lord, and Wait patiently for Him to act. Don't worry about evil people who prosper or fret about their wicked schemes.

Psalm 37 1: 8
Stop your anger! Turn from your rage! Do not envy others, it only leads to harm.

Your desires reveal your character. Whatever you desire reveals how you feel, how you think and what you want.

If you want to get anywhere in life you must desire and think positive.

There is nothing wrong with desires.

God desires the best for you and me.

He desires us to have good health, no pain, and whatever we do go through we put our trust in Him and become like Him.

God is motivated by His love for us. He provides the best for us.

You must ask is the desire consisted to what God wants for your life.

Sometimes people have the desire to be rich. There's nothing wrong with desiring money, but be careful for why you are asking for it.

1st Timothy 6: 9
But they that will be rich fall into temptation and a snare, and into many foolish and hurtful lusts, which drown men in destruction and perdition.

2nd Timothy 2: 9
And because I preach this Good News, I am suffering and have been chained like a criminal. But the word of God cannot be chained.

2nd Timothy 6: 10
I am willing to endure anything if it will bring salvation and eternal glory in Christ Jesus to those God has chosen.

Whatever desires are ungodly, will be corruptible and you will have a feeling of emptiness and destruction.

What are the requirements?

1. *Delight yourself in the Lord.*

    Do you love talking to Him?
    Do you love listening to Him?
    Do you love giving to Him?
    Do you love reading His Words?

    To delight in Him, you take pleasure in Him.

    It is not just the money you want you want a relationship with Him.

    He is interested in our love for Him.

    The more we look and act like Him in our spirit, He will pour out His blessing to us.

    If you delight yourself in Him your desires will be met.

    When you walk and talk with God to help you make the right choices and decisions, He will grant you what he chooses is best for you.

2. *Commit your way to the Lord.*

    Say Lord these are the desires of my heart, I commit myself to you.

    It always comes out better when you give it to God.

    Make sure you know that God is in charge not us.

3. *Trust in the Lord.*

    If you want the desires of your heart you must trust Him.

    If you want God's best, trust Him.

If He doesn't want someone or something in your like, trust Him. He knows what He's doing.

I will trust Him for the desires of my heart, because I know He knows what's best.

When I decide to do it myself without Him it comes out destructive or the consequences are not good.

4. *Rest in the Lord.*

It is easy for us to fret with God because He doesn't give us what we want when we want it.

The more intense our desire becomes, the more we fret. We become angry, and stop trusting God.

The Lord say lay it down. Rest in Him, Trust Him and He will move heaven and earth to give it to you.

If we don't trust in Him and start fretting over it, we are not being consistent with God and then we are disagreeing with Him.

5. *Wait Patiently for the Lord.*

The stronger we want something, we don't want to wait.

The Lord must have a reason for delaying what we want. Therefore we must say, Lord I am trusting you and waiting for you.

God is growing us up.

If we want His best we wait on Him.

Wait patiently. When we learn to put things in His hand we will be at peace.

God knows what you and I desire.

He knows and is much wiser than we.

Therefore we must delight ourselves in Him, Trust Him, wait patiently for Him and we will get God's best.

Let God give you what He wants you to have. Be patient and wait and you will have the best for you.

He will turn those disappointments into good.

It always comes out better when God's hand is in it.

Bible Study # 59
From the teaching of Anita Cameron
Amazing facts. Bibles are
The King James Version and
The New Believers Bible.

Destruction of The Earth

Will you be ready to meet Jesus in the sky?

KJV Isaiah 48: 3
Jesus said, "I have declared the former things from the beginning; and they went forth out of my mouth and I showed them; I did them suddenly, and they came to pass."

Isaiah 48: 16
Jesus said, "Mine hand also have laid the foundation of the earth, and my right hand has spanned the heavens; when I call them they stand up together."

Isaiah 48: 16
Jesus said. "Come you near unto me, hear you this; I have not spoken in secret from the beginning; from the time that it was, there I am now the Lord God, and His Spirit has sent me."

Isaiah 48: 17
Thus said the Lord, our Redeemer, The Holy One of Israel; I am the Lord your God which teach you to profit, which lead you by the way that you should go.

Isaiah 48:18
Jesus said. "O that you had hearkened to my commandments then had your peace been as a river and your righteousness as the waves of the sea."

Isaiah 48: 22
Jesus said, "There is no peace unto the wicked.

You as a believer in Christ Jesus know that God our Father sent His only begotten Son to earth as a living sacrifice.

Jesus came to earth born without sin through a virgin.

He walked the earth incorruptible, teaching, healing, raising up the dead and showing the wonderful kingdom of God.

Because of the sins of the earth, Jesus was the ultimate sacrifice.

He was crucified, after being bruised and beaten for our transgressions.

Jesus took all the sins of the earth upon Himself to free us from death.

He went down to hell and took the key of life back.

He took back the authority from Satan the devil that had been taken from Adam and Eve, and was resurrected back up to heaven to sit on the right hand side of our Father, giving authority and everlasting life for all who believe in Him.

Thereby enabling us to pray and ask for forgiveness when we fall short of His word.

Isaiah 48:8
States; that we were transgressors from the womb.

1st John 1: 9
Jesus forgives us if we confess our sins, He is faithful and just to forgives us of our sins.

We were born corruptible through sin, and the Lord's sacrifice has made us whole.

Through Jesus we can believe all things are possible, all power is in His hand, and he knows everything.

Thereby protecting us and giving us knowledge and wisdom to know that He's coming back and all that believe in Him shall not perish, but have everlasting life.

When the destruction to the Earth comes, greater is he that believes in Him, Because he will know that Jesus is coming back and His word is true.

All believers that are on earth will rise up to meet Him in the sky before He destroys the earth.

NBB Isaiah 24: 1
Look! The Lord is about to destroy the earth and make it a vast wasteland. See how He is scattering the people over the face of the earth.

Isaiah 24: 2
Priests and the people, servants and masters, maids and mistresses, buyers and sellers, lenders and borrowers, bankers and debtors, none will be spared.

Isaiah 24: 3
The earth will be completely emptied and looted. The Lord has spoken.

Isaiah 24: 4
The earth dries up, the crop withers, and the skies refuse to rain.

Isaiah 24: 5
The earth suffers for the sins of its people, for they have twisted the instructions of God, violated His laws, and broken His everlasting covenant.

Isaiah 24: 6
Therefore a curse consumes the earth and its people. They are desolate, destroyed by fire. Few will be left alive.

KJV Isaiah 2: 19
And they shall go into holes of the rocks, and into the caves of the earth for the fear of the Lord, and for the glory of His majesty, when He arises to shake terribly the earth.

Isaiah 2: 20
In that day a man shall cast his idols of silver, and his idols of gold, which they made each one for himself to worship, the moles and to the bats.

KJV Isaiah 24: 18
And it shall come to pass that he who flees from the noise of the fear shall fall into the pit. And he that comes out of the midst of the pit shall be taken in the snare: for the windows from on high are open, and the foundations of the earth do shake.

Amazing facts states: What will happen to sin and sinners?

Malachi 4: 1
All the proud, yes and all that do wickedly, shall be stubble: and that day come shall burn them up.

Revelation 20: 9
"Fire came down from God out of heaven and devoured them."

2nd Peter 3: 10
"The elements shall melt with fervent heat, the earth also and the works that are therein shall be burned up."

2nd Peter 3: 13
"Never the less we according to His promise, look for a new heavens and a new earth, wherein dwelled righteousness.

God will destroy all sin and sinners with fire. This fire will melt the earth and turn everything into ashes. Then God will make a perfect new earth, and the Holy City will be its capital. Here the righteous will live in joy, peace and holiness throughout eternity. God promises that sin will not rise up again.

Bible Study # 60
By Anita Cameron
Bibles: King James Version KJV) and
New Believers Bible (NBB).

Attached is the song I have written that was supernaturally given to me.

If You Do You're Child Of God

1. Do you walk by faith?

Hebrew 11: 1
Now faith is the substance of things hoped for, the evidence of things not seen.

Hebrew 12: 2
Looking unto Jesus the author and finisher of our faith; who for the joy that was set before Him endured the cross despising the shame, and set down at the right hand of the throne of God.

Romans 8: 28
We know that all things work together for good to them that love God, to them who are the called according to His purpose.

NBB Hebrew 12: 2
We do this by keeping our eyes on Jesus, on whom our Father depends from start to finish. He was willing to die a shameful death on the cross because of the joy He knew would be His afterward. Now He is seated in the place of highest honor on the right hand of God's throne in heaven.

Faith is believing in Jesus and that He is with you always. Faith is that you have no fear because He is always there.

When you walk out of your door you know He is with you, to take you wherever you are to go.

He has His angels around you to protect you.

Psalm 91: 11
For He shall give His angels charge over you to keep you in your way.

Faith acts, faith sees the answer, and faith put us beyond our sickness into healing.

Hebrew 11: 3
Through faith we understand that the worlds were framed by the word of God, so that things which are seen were not made of things which do appear.

Hebrew 11: 6
But without faith it is impossible to please God. For he that come to God must believe that He is and that He is rewarder of them that diligently seeks Him.

NBB 91:11
For He orders His angels to protect you wherever you go.

NBB 91: 12
They will hold you with their hands to keep you from striking your foot on a stone.

2. *Do you talk by faith?*

    Do you talk about your belief in Jesus?
    Do you testify about what He's done for you?
    Do you talk positive and believe?

3. *Do you praise His Holy grace?*

    Do you praise the Lord for His merciful grace, kindness and love He shows you everyday, not only when you're doing well but also when you're not doing so well?

4. *Do you pray by faith?*

    When you pray, do you believe it will be answered?
    It might not be answered when you want it, but He's always on time.

Do you believe He knows what's best for you, so when you pray His will, will be best for you? Because His power and wisdom knows the outcome of everything,
He wants the best for you.

5. *Do you praise Him everyday?*

   Every morning, during the day, in the evening, before you go to bed, do you praise and thank the Lord for His goodness, mercy and love He shows you everyday.

6. *Do you believe His words are true?*

   Do you read the bible and believe that the Holy Spirit is the author of the bible, and that He spiritually gave the writers what to write? He revealed to their memory their experience in the word of God. God is true and His words are true.

7. *Do you talk to Him everyday?*

   Do you meditate or just plainly talk to Jesus about what you want to do in life and how you feel, or do you just talk to Him about anything?

8. *Do you ask Him to guide your way?*

   Do you ask the Lord to guide you in decisions you have to make? Do you pray to Him asking Him for guidance because you know He knows what's best for you?

9. *Do you keep His words in your heart?*

   When you read the bible do you meditate on His words?

   NBB 1st John 2: 5
   But those who obey God's word really do love Him. That is the way to know whether or not we live in Him.

   KJV 1st John 2: 5
   But who so keep His word, in Him verily is the love of God perfected: hereby know we that we are in Him.

Do you keep a psalm in your heart and do you reflect on scriptures or versus in the bible?

10. *Do you worship and praise His name?*

Do you worship Him and praise His Holy Name, thanking Him for everything?

KJV Psalm 95: 6
O come let us worship and bow down: let us kneel before the Lord our maker.

NBB Psalm 95: 6
Come let us worship and bow down. Let us kneel before the Lord our maker, for He is our God.

NBB Psalm 94: 14
The Lord will not reject His people; He will not abandon His own special possession.

11. *Do you believe all power is in His hand?*

KJV Revelation 1: 8
I am alpha and omega, the beginning and the ending, said the Lord, which is, and which was, and which is to come, the almighty.

Jeremiah 51: 15
*He has made the earth by His **power**, He has established the world by His **wisdom**, and has stretched out heaven by His **understanding***

Jeremiah 51: 16
When He uttered His voice, there is a multitude of waters in the havens; and He caused the vapors to ascend from the ends of the earth: He makes lighting with rain, and brings forth the wind out of His treasures.

NBB Isaiah 40: 22
It is God who sits above the circle of the earth. The people below must seem to Him like grasshopper! He is the one who spreads out the heaven like a curtain and makes the tent from them.

Isaiah 40: 26
Look up into heaven. Who created all the stars? He brings them out one after another, calling each by its name, and He counts them to see that none are lost or have strayed away.

12. Do you believe He knows everything?

Jesus knew us before we were born. He knew us when we were in our mother's womb.

NBB Psalm 139: 1
O Lord you have examined my heart and know everything about me.

NBB Psalm 139: 2
You know when I sit down or stand up. You know my every thought when far away.

NBB Psalm 139: 3
You chart the path ahead of me and tell me where to stop and rest. Every moment you know where I am.

NBB Psalm 139: 4
You know what I am going to say even before I say it, Lord.

NBB Psalm 139: 5
You both precede and follow me. You place your hand of blessing on my head.

NBB Psalm 139; 6
Such knowledge is too wonderful for me and too great for me to know.

Psalm 139: 13
You made all the delicate, inner parts of my body. And knit me together in my mother's womb.

Psalm 139: 14
Thank you for making me so wonderfully complex! Your workmanship is marvelous and how well I know it.

Psalm 139: 15
You watched me as I was being formed in ulter seclusion, as I was woven together in the dark of the womb.

Psalm 139: 16
You saw me before I was born; everyday of my life was recorded in your book.

13. Do you believe He'll see you through, know matter what comes or what you go to?

What you are going through God already knew.

NBB 1ˢᵗ Corinthians 10: 13
But remember that the temptations that come into your life are no different from what others experience. And God is faithful; He will keep the temptation from becoming so strong that you can't stand against it. When you are tempted, He will show you a way out so that you will not give in to it.

Isaiah 40: 28
Have you not known, have you not heard the creator of the ends of the earth, fainted not neither is weary? There is no searching of His understanding.

Isaiah 40: 29
He gives power to the faint; and to them that have no might he increase strength.

Isaiah 40: 31
But they that wait on the Lord shall renew their strength; they shall mount up with wings as eagles; they shall run and not be weary; and shall walk and not faint.

14. Do you believe He has a plan for you?

The Spirit of God will enable you to do whatever God has plan for you.

Romans 8: 28
And we know that all things work together for good to them that love God, to them who are called according to His purpose.

Pastor John Cherry said,
While you were in your mother's womb, Jesus

1. He appointed parents for you before you were conceived.
2. He weaved a body around your spirit.
3. He gave you a time (a time to be born).
4. He gave you a gender (male or female).
5. He appointed you a race.
6. He appointed you times (span of time for each season of your life).
7. He appointed you a dwelling place (both naturally and spiritually).
8. He appointed you a day (determine whether you be with Him).
9. He determined your boundaries (physically and spiritually).
10. He will never give you more than you can bear.

15. *Do you believe He died to save you?*

Ephesians 2: 8
For by grace are you saved through faith; and that not of yourselves: It is the gift of God.

Do you believe that God the Father sent His only begotten Son Jesus down to earth to be the ultimate sacrifice for the sins of the world, so that those who believe in Him will have everlasting life? Jesus died for us, He was beaten and bruised. His pain was unimaginable.

16. *Do you believe you are redeemed?*

Jesus came to redeem mankind. He came to be a ransom for us to save us from our sins. He took away our sins. We are now redeemed.

17. *Do you believe He is our Christ, God and King?*

If you believe everything from the beginning of the bible study, then you are a child of God.

Song written by Anita Joy Cameron
5/25/07
These Words Were Super Naturally Given to me.

"If you do, you're child of God?"

Do you walk, walk by faith?"
Do you talk, talk by faith?
Do you praise His Holy Grace?
If you do, you're a child of God.

Do you pray, pray by faith?
Do you praise Him everyday?
Do you believe His words are true?
If you do, you're a child of God.

Do you talk, talk to Him everyday?
Do you ask Him to guide your way?
Do you keep His words in your heart?
If you do, you're a child of God.

Do you worship and praise His name?
Do you believe all power is in His hand?
Do you believe He knows everything?
If you do, you're a child of God.

Do you believe He'll see you through?
Know matter what comes or what you go to?
Do you believe He has a plan for your life?
If you do, you're a child of God.

Do you believe He died to save you?
Do you believe you are redeemed?
Do you believe He is our God, Christ and King?
If you do, you're a child of God.

Table of Contents

1. Are you Limiting God's Blessing 243
2. Landmine of Compromise 248
3. Unforgiving Spirit 252
4. Spirit Of Fear 256
5. Landmine of Sexual Sin 260
6. A Good Conscience 264
7. Condition of a Conscience 268
8. Facing our Loneliness 273
9. Our Trustworthy Guide 276
10. Faith in Life's Fire 281
11. Release From the Bondage of Rejection 285
12. It's Good to Give thanks to God 290
13. Controlling your Thoughts 294
14. God's call to Genuine Repentance 296
15. A Realtor for the Lord 301

Bible Study # 61
From the teaching of Dr. Charles Stanley
Also input by Anita Cameron.
Bible: King James Version (KJV) and
New Believer's Bible (NBB)

Are You Limiting God's Blessing?

Are there needs in your life that you feel are not being met?

Are their desires that you feel are not being met?

You believe in God and you are trying to do the right things in life, yet things don't seem to happen for you.

When you pray, do you believe in getting an answer, and are you preparing for your answer?

Discover why our needs and desires are not being met.

God delights in doing well for us.

He promises to provide those things when we hear Him and listen to Him.

Psalm 81: 10
For it was I, the Lord your God, Who rescued you from the land of Egypt. Open your mouth wide and I will fill it with good things.

*Psalm **81:11***
"But no, my people wouldn't listen! Israel did not want me around.

Psalm 81: 12
So I let them follow their blind and stubborn way, living according to their own desires.

Psalm 81: 13
But oh, that my people would listen to me! Oh, that Israel would follow me, walking in my paths.

Psalm 81: 16
The Lord said, "I would feed you with the best of foods. I would satisfy you with wild honey from the rock."

Do you want God's best in your life, or do you want what you feel is best for you?

Philippians 4: 19
And this same God who takes care of me will supply all your needs from His glorious riches, which have been given to us in Christ Jesus.

God does not want you to want the bear necessities.

God is a God who desires to bless us.

Psalm 23:1
The Lord is my shepherd I shall not want.

You should worship one God and one God only.

Psalm 145: 18
The Lord is close to all that call on Him, yes, to all who calls on Him sincerely.

Psalm 145: 19
He fulfills the desires of those who fear Him; He hears their cries for help and rescues them.

Do we pray and really believe in Him?

Psalm 103: 1
Praise the Lord I tell myself; with my whole heart, I will praise His holy name.

Psalm 103: 2
Praise the Lord, I tell myself, and never forget the good things He does for me.

Psalm 103: 3
He forgives all my sins and heals all my diseases.

Psalm 103: 4
He ransoms me from death and surrounds me with love and tender mercies.

Psalm 103: 5
He fills my life with good things. My youth is renewed like the eagles

Psalm 103: 5
The Lord gives righteousness and justice to all who are treated unfairly.

He loves us and provides our every need.

God's very best for you are not the same plan
He has for someone else life.

We get His best by our response to Him and our trust in Him.

God does not change; He has a desire to bless every one of us.

1. *When you ask God to meet your needs you must be specific.*

    a. Ask step by step of what you want.
    b. If you want a husband or wife, you must list all the qualities you want he or she to have.
    c. Do not ask for something that is not of God? *For ex*: Something belonging to someone else.
    d. If He tells you no, He has something better for you.

    Every time God has moved throughout my life, He's given me something better.

2. *Anticipate and expect an answer from God.*

    a. Make preparation for what you ask of God, because you anticipate God will give you an answer.

3. *Learn to wait on God's timing.*

    a. When God does not do it right away, don't go off feeling that you can't wait and start comparing yourself with others and what they have.

    God has the best for you.

    A believer can have idols. Therefore, remove the idols from your life.

    When you are in the process of making a decision do you base it on the will of someone else, instead of the will of God?

    There is One God Jehovah, Jesus His Son, our savior and the Holy Spirit who governs the word of God.

4. *Trust God for something big that you cannot do yourself.*

    a. The more impossible it is the more God enjoys.
    b. Open your mouth wide and ask big, expect big.

    He wants to work in our lives so that people will know that the God you believe in is God.

5. *Walk in the ways of the Lord by living in obedience.*
6. *Don't live in the past.*

    You say, "God show me what is hindering your best for me.

    God show me if I have idols in my life where I let or I am concerned about what others think."

    You surrender to God and say God I want to be clean.

    From that moment on let God show you the best He has in store for you.

    He will cleanse and honor you.

1st Peter 4: 10
God has given gifts to each of you from His great variety of spiritual gifts. Manage them well so that God's generosity can flow through you.

God blesses us so that we can bless others

No matter how successful you are you would not be there without God. And God blesses others so that they can bless you.

Bible Study # 62
From the teachings of Dr. Charles Stanley
Input also by Anita Cameron
Bible: King James Version (KJV)

Landmines of Compromise

Learn how to avoid and identify life's danger.

Anytime you compromise with evil, evil wins.

Lets take a look at King Solomon.

2nd Chronicles 1:1
Solomon the son of David was strengthened in his kingdom, and the Lord his God was with him, and magnified him exceedingly.

1st King 10: 23
So King Solomon exceeded all the kings of the earth for riches and wisdom.

1st King 10: 24
And all the earth sought Solomon, to hear his wisdom, which God had put in his heart.

God gave Solomon the privilege of building His temple.

1st King 11: 1
But Solomon loved many strange women, together with the daughter of Pharaoh, woman of Moabites, Ammonites, Edomities, Jidonians, and Hittites.

1st King 11: 2
Of nation concerning which the Lord said unto the children of Israel, you shall not go into them, neither shall they come in unto you: For surely they will turn away your heart after their gods: Solomon cleave unto these in love.

1ˢᵗ king 11: 4
For it came to pass, when Solomon was old, that his wives turned away his heart after other gods: and his heart was not perfect with the Lord his God, as was the heart of David his father.

What happened to Solomon was that by not following God's word he became like them. He compromised.

We as believers should not be in the company of unbelievers, because we can compromise our morals.

The first step of compromise is the most dangerous of them all.

Compromise work where things don't seem that bad.

You say, "Everybody's doing it." And you take that little step and then the next thing you know you are out of the ream of God.

Going to a party and you are offered a drink or to do something you don't do and shouldn't be doing, and you say no. That person will tell you, "Just try it, try a little, it won't hurt you, join the party."

That person is a person with no conviction. A person with no conviction is dangerous.

Just because you don't participate it doesn't make you less than; it makes you stronger than.

When you compromise and violate your conscience you are going against your conviction to listen to the Holy Spirit.

How many people have you heard say, "If only I had listened."

You knew not to be in the company of certain individuals but you did it anyway.

When you do things and violate your God given conviction, these unbelievers don't respect you, they talk about you and say, "See I told you she/he is a fake. They are not all that. They talk about being a Christian, but they did this and they did that."

We live in a world that a little of this and a little of that and if it's wrong, it will eventually destroy you.

If your friends want you to participate in something that's wrong they are not your friends. Also if your friends are trying to make you feel bad because of your godly life, you don't need friends like that either.

It is a compromise for a believer to be bound together with an unbeliever.

Before a person gets married, they should make sure they are marrying a believer of God and His word.

When you live godly you will be subject to ridicule, but God has all power, and He alone can do anything for you. They can't.

Do you have the courage to stand up for your convictions to God?

Know matter how you feel if God says it's not right, it's not right.

Compromise works like this: you are asked to do something that seems not to terribly wrong. It's either right or wrong, there is no in between.

Do you have standards to live by?

A person with no moral standards and basic biblical beliefs will be able to do anything without feelings, are regards for others. The same thing is true about money and relationships,

When a believer back slide, it doesn't make them unsaved its makes them dirty. Then they began to desensitize their conscience.

When you desensitize your conscience you will go farther and farther away from your convictions of God and you will find yourself without a conscience, then anything goes.

Some people feel if they don't participate, they don't belong.

Do you choose to obey God and have His favor, or do you choose to have favor of others who don't have any power?

The most important relationship you have is with Jesus Christ.

When we go another way, we lose our fellowship with Him.

We must have an intimate relationship with God. So that we don't be like the unbelievers, they are always trying to fill their void.

Obedience to God is the satisfaction in your life. It enables you by the Holy Spirit to say no.

Consequence of Compromising

1. You lose your intimate relationship with God.
2. When you stand strong against compromising you might lose friends and family.

How to avoid compromising yourself

1. Make the word of God a standard for your conduct. (The Ten Commandments).
2. Begin everyday to read the Bible and get on your knees to pray.
3. Obey the initial prompting of the Holy Spirit.

People will say, "Where in the bible does it say you should not drink.

When the Holy Spirit says no, you should say no.

Don't say I am going to think about it. When you do that you are opening yourself up to compromise and you are not listening to the Holy Spirit.

But when you do compromise and mess up, you should pray with sincerity:

"Lord I have messed up, Please God I am asking you to forgive me of my sins and enable me to be in the power of the Holy Spirit to say NO."

The Lord will forgive you.

Bible Study # 63
From the teaching of Dr Charles Stanley
Input also by Anita Cameron
Bible: King James Version (KJV) and
New Beginners Bible (NBB)

Unforgiving Spirit

It is never the will of God to have an unforgiving spirit in you.

No matter what we may think or feel, it is not God's will for us to be unforgiving to anyone.

We want to go by our feelings and what we think or what others think. We always want people to feel sorry for us by relating what people have done to us.

Unforgiveness is a person's willful denial to refuse to lay down resentment, anger, and hostility they have for someone.

When a person keeps unforgivness in their heart it is rebelling against the word of God, because it tares you up inside and out, and it is destructive by nature.

When we let God in our life, we cannot have an unforgiving spirit inside of us.

We cannot defend an unforgiving spirit because any reason is unacceptable.

If a person is a believer of God, being unforgiving is out of character.

Unforgiving is self-destructive, it is a form of bondage. It keeps you in a state of mind that is unhealthy, and that's exactly where Satan wants you to be.

If you don't want to live your life in bondage then you must forgive. No one said you had to forget, but by you forgiving it frees you and brings you peace.

If you say you cannot forgive them no matter what, then you will never be free and have peace.

There are also people who have to forgive themselves. Some people think about what they have done in the past and they feel that since it was so horrible, they can never forgive themselves.

Jesus paid the sin death for the entire world. When you ask Jesus to forgive you He forgives you. Remember He died to save us and took away all our sins. He redeemed us, now it is up to us to take part in His saving grace and forgive ourselves.

NBB Ephesians 4: 26
And "don't sin by letting anger gain control over you." Don't let the sun go down while you are still angry.

NBB **Ephesians 4: 27**
For anger gives a mighty foothold to the devil.

NBB Ephesians 4: 28
If you are a thief, stop stealing, begin using your hands for honest work, and then give generously to others in need.

NBB Ephesians 4: 29
Don't use foul or abusive language. Let everything you say be good and helpful, so that your words will be an encouragement to those who hear them.

NBB Ephesians 4: 30
And do not bring sorrow to God's Holy Spirit by the way you live. Remember He is the one who has identified you as His own guaranteeing that you will be saved on the day of redemption.

NBB Ephesians 4: 31
Get rid of all bitterness, rage, anger, harsh words, and slander as well as all types of malicious behavior.

NBB Ephesians 4: 32
Instead, be kind to each other, tenderhearted, forgiving one another, just as God through Christ has forgiven you.

There are many people who live for animosity. They are always looking to pay somebody back for something.

KJV Romans 12: 19
Dearly beloved, avenge not you, but rather give place unto wrath. For it is written, VENGEANCE is mind, I will repay, said the Lord.

We must be willing to let Him handle it.

KJV Matthew 18:21
Then came Peter and said, Lord how often shall my brother sin against me, and I forgive Him? Till seven times?

KJV Matthew 18: 22
Jesus said unto Him. I say not unto thee, until seven times; but until seventy times seven.

Consequences of not forgiving

1. A person will look and appear sad because it begins working on their spirit, heart, and mind. If anyone listening to there conversation will see that they have something tearing on the inside of them. It affects their life.
2. Affects Relationships: There's no joy, happiness, peace and they are sometime sad and somber.
3. Affects human body, cheating and bitterness: You better think twice before you get marry, because you have to wonder how much anger and resentment will that person bring in to the marriage from their past relationships.
4. Affects Your Worship: You will not keep in your heart and minds that as the Father forgives you, so shall you forgive others.
5. Short-circuit Your Faith: You start doubting God's word.
6. Your Whole Perspective on life gets warp: You begin to feel there's no hope and feel lost.

How should you deal with your unforgiving spirit?

Acknowledge your unforgiving spirit and identify that person, and say "God I am asking you to help me lay it down. I choose to no longer have an unforgiving spirit.

With the power of the Holy Spirit with us, we can have peace and joy we cannot explain.

When you ask God to come into your life as your Lord and savior, the Holy Spirit will come into your life and He will commune with you, guide you, comfort you, reveal things to you, empower you, teach you, council you and bring things to your memory.

Bible Study # 64
From the teaching of Dr. Charles Stanley
Input also by Anita Cameron
New Beginners Bible (NNB)

Spirit Of Fear

God does not give us the spirit of fear. He doesn't want us to have any fear.

NBB Isaiah 41: 4
Who has done such mighty deeds, directing the affairs of the human race as each new generation marches by: It is the Lord the First the Last. I alone am He.

NBB Isaiah 41: 10
Don't be afraid, for I am with you. Do not be dismayed, for I am your God. I will strengthen you. I will help you. I will uphold you with my victorious right hand.

NBB Isaiah 41: 13
I am holding you by your right hand, I, the Lord your God. And I say to you "Do not be afraid. I am here to help you."

I am not talking about fear of touching a hot stove because you know you will get burned. I am not talking about fear of running into a bear in the woods, where you know the outcome could be dangerous.

I am not talking about things you know for example it's good to fear drugs and alcohol because the outcome of using these drugs is dangerous.

I am talking about fear that is inwardly.

We all have a recorder in our brain that records everything that happens to us that causes us fear.

A mother who has been hurt by men will probably tell her daughter do not trust men.

A person with phobias will continue to record over and over their fears.

Source of Fear

1. The Imagination a Shadow Affect: People who imagine things are accruing in their life or things that might happen.

   A person might fear leaving the house because they image something is going to happen to them.

2. Ignorance of Spiritual Things: A person that is ignorant of God's words that all sins are forgiven by God because He died for us.
3. Doubting the Promises of God: A person that doubts the promises of God that He provides all our needs.
4. A Poor Self-image: When a parent or other children criticize a person and tells them they are ugly or stupid, it gets on their recorder and they began to think they are ugly and stupid. Fear sets in because of what others say about them.

Fear Creates

1. Tension: The environment will not be peaceful. In time when a person becomes fearful anxiety takes over.

   When anxiety occur it do not fit who we are because we are children of God. He has all power, knows all, and is everywhere.

   The key to getting rid of fear is in the word of God.

NBB Ephesians 1: 3
Blessed be the God and Father of our Lord Jesus Christ, who has blessed us with all spiritual blessing in heavenly places in Christ.

NBB Ephesians 1: 4
According as He has chosen us in Him before the foundation of the world, that we should be holy and without blame before Him in love.

NBB Ephesians 1: 5
Having predestined us unto the adoption of children by Jesus Christ to Himself according to the pleasure of His will.

God said to Moses, Joshua, Gideon and to us His children,

"I chose you; I will be with you.
I will strengthen you.
I am your God.
Surely I will help you."

God who is JEHOVAH GOD is in control of all things.

Fear Creates

2. Procrastination: People are afraid to try something for fear of failing.
3. Inability to Achieve in life: Not having the courage to deal with the outside world.

NBB Joshua 1: 9
I command you be strong and courageous! Do not be afraid or discouraged. For the Lord your God is with you wherever you go.

4. Damage your self-esteem and self-image: Satan and your inner recorder goes off that you are a failure, you can't do it.
5. You feel rejection and isolation in relationships: a person will feel its better not to become friends with anyone.
6. You oftentimes panic and make wrong decisions.
7. It affects your physical health.

Proverbs 17: 22
A cheerful heart is good medicine, but a broken spirit saps a person's strength.

Isaiah 64: 4
For since the world began, no ears have heard, and no eye has seen a God like you, who works for those who wait for Him.

God's doing the holding, we do not have to worry or be afraid of anything.

Identify the fear and say "Father I thank you and by the power of the Holy Spirit in me, I choose to lay it down."

Will it pop up again? Yes, the devil will bring it up into your mind.

Meditate Daily for 3 weeks on Isaiah 41: 9-13

Isaiah 41: 9
I have called you back from the ends of the earth so you can serve me. For I have chosen you and will not throw you away.

Isaiah 41: 10
Don't be afraid for I am with you. Do not dismay, for I am your God. I will strengthen you. I will help you. I will uphold you with my victorious right hand.

Isaiah 41: 11
See all your angry enemies lie there, confused and ashamed. Anyone who opposes you will die.

Isaiah 41: 12
You will look for them in vain. They will all be gone!

Isaiah 41: 13
I am holding you by your right hand. I, the Lord your God. And I say to you, "Do not be afraid. I am here to help you."

Bible Study # 65
From the teaching of Dr. Charles Stanley
Input also by Anita Cameron.
Bible: New Beginners Bible (NBB)

Landmine of Sexual Sin

We live in a very sensual society. We have lived in this so long we compromise for what's going on.

We allow unbelievers to redefine morality.

1st Thessalonians 4: 3
God wants you to be holy, so you should keep clear of all sexual sin.

1st Thessalonians 4: 4
Then each of you will control your body and live in holiness and honor,

1st Thessalonians 4: 5
not in lustful passion as the pagans do, in their ignorance of God and His ways.

1st Thessalonians 4: 6
Never cheat a Christian brother in this matter by taking His wife, for the Lord avenges all such sins, as we have solemnly warned you before.

1st Thessalonians 4: 7
God has called us to be holy, not to live impure lives.

1st Thessalonians 4: 8
Anyone who refuses to live by these rules is not disobeying human rules but is rejecting God, who gives His Holy Spirit to you.

When a man and woman meet it should not be for lust. It should be two people getting to know one another intimately.

Love is I want what's best for you.

Lust is I want what's best for me.

No man should transgress against His brother, in other words you do not take someone else's husband or wife.

Sex was created for us for pleasure not lust.

Lust is getting us out of what God intended it to be.

God gave us the Holy Spirit to guide us.

Anyone cannot do anything to His body.

1st Corinthians 6: 19
Don't you know that your body is the temple of the Holy Spirit, who lives in you and was given to you by God? You do not belong to yourself.

1st Corinthians 6: 20
For God bought you with a high price, so you must honor God with your body.

Sexual sins began in our mind, though, imagination and a choice consent.

1st Corinthians 10: 13
But remember that the temptations that come into your life are no different from others experience. And God is faithful He will keep the temptation from becoming so strong that you can't stand up against it. When you are tempted, He will show you a way out so that you will not give into it.

Satan gets a strong hold in your life when you disobey God.

Once one gives over to sexual sin, intimacy is lost.

As long as you're caught up in lust, you will never have an intimate relationship with God or anyone.

The power of temptation is deceptive offer of immediate pleasure without penalty, and that is a devil's lie. Unbelief cannot utter the truth.

What causes sexual immorality?

1. Control—Why does an adult sexually molest children?
2. Acceptance—People want to feel they are accepted and wanted.
3. Intimacy—Is find, but when it gets out of boundaries, it's not good.
4. Desire to conquer—A person was hurt by someone and out of anger wants to get even.
5. Financial—To get financial security, but you're only a sophisticated prostitute.

You ask yourself, "am I going into this relationship in truth?"

Consequences in disobeying God.

1. Guilt, condemnation and anxiety.
2. A divided mind—It demise your capacity.
3. Damage of self-image.
4. Emptiness.
5. Loneliness.
6. Disappointment.
7. Depression.
8. Doubt
9. Diseases—There's no exception to the laws of God.
10. Broken homes.

This sin builds a wall between you and God. All sins grieve the heart of God.

How to deal with sexual immorality?

1. Confess your adulterous act.
2. Acknowledge and take responsibility.
3. Genuinely repent.
4. Pray for God's forgiveness.

If we confess our sin He's faithful and just.

He died on the cross to cleanse us from all sin and uncleanness.

6. We have to forgive ourselves.
7. Seek wide godly counsel to help you forgive yourself. You have damaged your whole emotional system.
8. Walk away from it—Separate yourself from that relationship.

When you walk away they usually find someone else.

If they are true they will turn to God.

9. Read God's word daily.

Psalm 119: 9
How can a young person stay pure? By obeying your word and following the rules.

Proverbs 4: 23
Above all else guard your heart, for it affects everything you do.

Proverbs 4: 25
Look straight ahead and fix your eyes on what lies before you.

Proverbs 4: 26
Mark out a straight path for your feet then stick to the path and stay safe.

Proverbs 4: 27
Don't get sidetracked; keep your feet from following evil.

God's way of comforting us, and showing us His way, is the way.

Bible Study # 66
From the teaching of Dr. Charles Stanley
Input also by Anita Cameron
Bible: New Beginners Bible (NBB)

"A Good Conscience"

God has given everyone a conscience whether you are a Christian or not.

A conscience deals with what's right and what's wrong.

A person after awhile will confess because of their conscience.

Its things we know are wrong because of our conscience.

In any society it is known that rape, murder, stealing lying and adultery is wrong.

Romans 1: 18
But God shows His anger from heaven against all sinful, wicked people who push the truth away from themselves.

Romans 1: 19
For the truth about God is known to them instinctively. God has put this knowledge in their hearts.

Romans 1: 20
From the time the world was created people have seen the earth and sky and all that God made. They can clearly see His invisible qualities, His eternal power and divine nature. So they have no excuse whatsoever for not knowing God.

God has made Himself so well known, even people who don't want to believe know that certain sins that are committed there's a penalty.

Sooner or later sin pays off. What you sow, so shall you reap.

Even people making movies know that the sinners get caught at the end.

Having a conscience is a gift from God. When you violate it, it gets duller and duller and the next thing you know, you're over the line and the wages for sin is death.

When you sin against God, you have felt it.

Romans 1: 24
So God let them go ahead and do whatever shameful things their hearts desired. As a result, they did vile and degrading things with each other's bodies.

Romans 1: 25
Instead of believing what they knew was the truth about God; they deliberately chose to believe lies. So they worshipped the things God made but not the Creator Himself, who is to be, praised forever Amen.

When you dull your conscience down, you change the truth of God into a lie.

The last thing we want God to do is give us over to our sin.

Romans 1: 26
That is why God abandoned them to their shameful desires. Even the woman turned against the natural way to have sex and instead indulged in sex with each other.

Romans 1: 27
And the men, instead of having normal sexual relationships with women, burned with lust for each other. Men did shameful things with other men and as a result suffered within themselves the penalty they so richly deserved.

Romans 1: 28
When they refused to acknowledge God, He abandoned them to their evil minds and let them do things that should never be done.

God gives common grace: He loves what He has created but He puts divine restraints. A person out there can do a lot of evil things but God has put divine restraints therefore, He will not let them go but so far.

God's standard is the Ten Commandments.

The Holy Spirit is not your conscience.

A lot of people think the Holy Spirit is their conscience, He is not. God gave everybody his or her own conscience.

Only when you accept Jesus as your Lord and savior,
then you will receive
The Holy Spirit.

The Holy Spirit then deals with your conscience.
He guides us in all truth.

It is very clear every single person has a conscience given to them by God. It monitors what you think and everything you do.

The word of God sharpens your conscience. It shows us what to do, to distinguish between right and wrong.

Your conscience has been programmed.

A parent that programs their child the word of God, the child knows to respond in a certain way.

It is very important that parents teach their children what's right and what's wrong.

When a child is not programmed properly, they will be programmed improperly.

Your conscience is not your guide.

The Holy Spirit helps us to:

1. Understand, and He interprets the signal.
2. Brings spiritual principals to mind.
3. Warns us of the consequence. When we violate our conscience, He urges us to make the right decision.
4. Empower you to say "NO."

We need to read the bible it speaks to our conscience.

Sin pays horrible wages.

God gives us a conscience as a gift to protect us.

Your conscience:

1. Affects your prayer life.
2. It affects your relationship with others.
3. If you choose to use your conscience wrongly, your conscience will be come duller and dark. Thereby enabling Satan to take hold over you.

Let your conscience be your guide and let The Holy Spirit guide your conscience.

Bible Study # 67
From the teaching of Dr. Charles Stanley
Input also by Anita Cameron
Bible: NBB New Beginners Bible

Condition of a Conscience—Part 2

The Purpose for having a conscience is protection.

1st Peter 3: 13
Now who will want to harm you if you are eager to do good?

1st Peter 3: 14
But even if you suffer for doing what is right, God will reward you for it. So don't be afraid and don't worry.

1st Peter 3: 15
Instead, you must worship Christ as Lord of your life and if you are asked about your Christian hope, always be ready to explain it.

1st Peter 3: 16
But you must do this in a gentle and respectful way keep your conscience clear. Then if people speak evil against you, they will be ashamed when they see what a good life you live because you belong to Christ.

Apostle Paul said, "After God changed his life, he began to live right with God."

We have let others program our conscience; our teachers, parents, minister and peers have a lot do with it.

That why it's important to teach and guide children correctly.

There are seven different words related to conscience.

1. A Good Conscience—a conscience where you fear God and don't do things that are against His will. A good conscience has nothing to say.
2. A Blameless Conscience—Your conscience isn't blaming you.

Acts 24: 14
But I admit that I follow the way, which they call a sect. I worship the God of our ancestors, and I firmly believe the Jewish Law and everything written in the book of prophecy.

Acts 24: 15
I have hope in God, just as these men do, that He will raise both the righteous and ungodly.

Acts 24: 16
Because of this; I always try to maintain a clear conscience before God and everyone else.

3. A Clear Conscience—I don't compromise my convictions. Our conscience is there in order to protect us.
4. A Weak Conscience—We all know there's one God, but some people participate in things and then feel guilty after.

1st Corinthians 8: 4
So now what about it? Should we eat meat that has been sacrificed to idols? Well, we all know that an idol is not really a god and that there is only one God and no other.

1st Corinthians 8: 5
According to some people, there are many so-called gods and many lords, both in heaven and on earth.

1st Corinthians 8: 6
But we know that there is only one God, the Father, who created everything, and we exist for Him. And there is only one Lord, Jesus Christ, through whom God made everything and through whom we have been given life.

We have to guard our conscience; because people watch us and we influence them.

5. A Defiled Conscience—When a person sins against God, they defile their conscience. Their conscience gets dirty, dusty and dimmer and dimmer. Eventually they don't even realize its dark and therefore their testimony of God is not even heard.

Titus 1: 15
Everything is pure to those whose hearts are pure. But nothing is pure to those who are corrupt and unbelieving, because their minds and consciences are defiled.

6. An Evil Conscience—A person will do something to someone no matter what it cost.

A person with an evil conscience is going to suffer the awful consequence.

Hebrew 10: 22
Let us go right into the presence of God's people, with true hearts fully trusting Him. For our evil conscience have been sprinkled with Christ's blood to make us clean, and our bodies have been washed with pure water.

7. A Seared Conscience—Sin has hardened their conscience. They are not listening because they are no longer hearing.

1st Timothy 4: 1
Now the Holy Spirit tells us clearly that in the last times some will turn away from what we believe; they will follow lying spirits and teachings that come from demons.

1st Timothy 4: 2
These teachers are hypocrites and liars. They pretend to be religious, but their consciences are dead.

Your Conscience should be Clear, Blameless and Clean.

When your conscience is clear, blameless and clean:

1. You will bear the fruit of courage in difficult times.
2. Gives you peace in your heart.

    One of the most powerful weapons is to remain in the capacity of calmness when the weapons come.

3. You are fearless.

    There's no fear, you have your heavenly Father on your side.

    There is power and boldness in a clear conscience—you are standing on the platform of truth.

Can you trust your conscience?

1. You must trust Jesus Christ as your personal savior.
2. The word of God must be your standard for living.
3. You must allow no contradictions to the word of God.
4. You must surrender to The Holy Spirit.

    I am trusting The Holy Spirit to guide me. His way is the best way.

    It is foolish to try to live without The Holy Spirit.

5. Requires daily cleansing.

How can you clean a dirty conscience?

There is no way we can do it.

But, if we confess to Jesus Christ our sins, in sincerity, and be in agreement with Him that we did it wrong.

God knows your heart. He knows your heart and everything about you and He knows the sincerity of your heart.

If you keep sinning and confessing continually, eventually it won't mean a thing.

When you confess you must repent.

If God tells you to clear your conscience with someone and you make excuses for not doing so, then your conscience is not clear.

If something is bothering you from years ago, your conscience is not clear.

Ask God to forgive you.

I want you to have a clean, clear and blameless conscience and you will have an awesome surety, peace, harmony and assurance.

How do we rid ourselves of guilt?

Ask Jesus Christ for forgiveness.

Obey God and leave all consequences to Him.

Otherwise you will live a life of fear, depression, shame, worthlessness and always the threat of punishment.

Bible Study # 68
From the teachings of Dr. Charles Stanley
Input also by Anita Cameron
Bible: King James Version (KJV) and
New Beginners Bible (NBB)

Facing our Loneliness

God does not want us to be lonely.

Loneliness is being disconnected.

It causes anxiety, and affects your life in a negative way.

The difference between loneliness and solitude is that solitude is a choice to be alone
and loneliness is a feeling of being without.

Solitude is good. All of us need time to be alone. Alone with the Father or be alone with ourselves.

Loneliness is not a matter of geography, but a matter of attitude. Loneliness can be found anywhere.

Loneliness began with Adam and Eve. When they chose to disobey God and obey Satan, they were taking out of the Garden of Eden and place in an unknown environment; An environment where they had to toil for themselves.

Loneliness is caused by

1. The death of someone.
2. Divorce or separation.
3. Lack of relationships;

A person that has built a wall around themselves to prevent them from being hurt again.

4. Feeling condemned by God: They do not ask for forgiveness.
5. Unworthiness: A poor self-image. They feel know body likes them and know one wants to be in their presents.

> It will affect their life in the way they treat people. They will not be able to love.

6. No one to share the joy in their life: They feel "Who wants to listen to me and who cares?"
7. Distorted of themselves; they see themselves as being ugly.
8. Childhood experiences; Insecurities, and the feeling of being not wanted and loved by parents or by God.

> It is very important that parents teach their children, starting at a very young age, that God loves them and He will never leave them.

> Teach them *Proverbs* 3: 5 and 6

> *KJV Proverbs 3: 5*
> Trust in the Lord with all your heart; and lean not unto your own understanding.

> *KJV Proverbs 3: 6*
> In all your way acknowledge Him, and He shall direct thy paths.

> *NBB Proverbs 3: 5*
> Trust in the Lord with all your heart; do not depend on your understanding.

> *NBB Proverbs 3: 6*
> Seek His will in all you do, and He will direct your path.

Consequences of Loneliness in life

1. It can kill you.
2. Affects your moral life.
3. Affects how you dress.

> When a woman plunge her blouse line, she wants to be seen. She wants attention.

The way to get attention is to be godly; being godly means to be kind and gentle.

4. Affects your finances: A person shopping thinks that it takes away their loneliness.
5. Affects how you eat: A person trying to comfort himself or herself will either overeat or become unhappy with their eating habits.
6. Affects relationships.
7. Affects a person health.
8. Divides the mind: A person is always undecided.
9. Drives people to drink.
10. Drives a person to multiple sexual affairs.
11. Constant make changes.

There is one source to keep you in Jesus Christ.

How do you handle it.

It began with being reconciled with God your creator.

God loves you. He gave His only begotten Son to save you.

The Holy Spirit will guide you out of that loneliness and get you to walk in peace, joy and hominy.

Always keep in your heart and mind that you are never alone. God the Father, God the Son Jesus, and God the Holy Spirit is always with you.

Bible Study # 69
From the teaching of Dr. Charles Stanley
Input also by Anita Cameron
Bible: King James Version and
New Beginners Bible (NBB)

Our Trustworthy Guide

Whosoever is guiding you must know your path because you are the only person that has to take that path.

Are you on the path that God has decided for you? Or are you letting others decide your path.

Look at the world we live in. There is a lot of hurt, deceit, crime, fear and lust.

People use sexual things to make money and they have taken over the world with the idea that it is right and acceptable.

When you see cheerleaders making sexual moves in their cheers for their team it looks gross, but people accept it and say! "Oh that's' how things are now. This is a new generation and they think differently."

Think about how many people that have been guided to believe that using sex to sell anything is okay.

Do you realize being guided by someone on that trail is leading you to destruction?

Psalm 32: 8
The Lord says, "I will guide you along the best pathway for your life. I will advise you and watch over you.

Psalm 32: 9
Do not be like a senseless horse or mile that needs a bit and bridle to keep it under control."

Here is a simple warning and challenge: a lot of people feel they can do it on their own. They make their own decision and feel that they can guide their own life.

God is available to all that wants to be available to Him.

When you see you have taken the wrong path say,

Psalm 31: 3
You are my rock and my fortress, for the honor of your name, lead me out this peril.

Psalm 48: 3
God Himself is in Jerusalem's tower. He reveals Himself as her defender.

Psalm 73: 23
Yet I still belong to you; you are holding my right hand.

Psalm 73: 24
You will keep on guiding me with your counsel.

Do you have a guide, but do it your way?

We all need a guide because we are inadequate to live out this life that God has planned for us.

There are a lot of people that seem to be doing well. They do what they want, go where they want to go. Spend money as they please, but do they have a relationship with God.

Luke 12: 16-19
There was this rich man, who had a fertile farm that produced fine crops: In fact His barns were full to overflowing. So he said, "I know! I'll tear down my barn and build bigger ones: Then I will have room to store everything and I'll sit back and say to myself, my friend, you have enough stored away for years to come. Now take it easy! Eat, drink and be merry!"

Luke 12: 20-21
But God said to him "you fool! You will die this very night, then who will get it all? Yes a person is a fool to store up earthly wealth but not have a rich relationship with God.

When you make a decision to live a life without God, God says you are a fool.

That's why we all need a guide our spiritual guide Jesus.

Psalm 32: 8
Jesus said, "I will instruct thee and teach thee in the way which you shall go. I will guide you with mine eyes.

Jesus said I will never leave you or forsake you and I will counsel you in not marrying or have a relationship with a person.

Have you ignored God, and doing it your way, or are you being mislead by others?

Only God knows you, He said "I will counsel you with my eyes on you."

He knows Our Personality, our strength, our weakness, our desires, our relationships, and what we should watch out for. Why not follow the one who knows all about us.

None of us know ourselves perfectly. Almighty God knows us perfectly.

The reason for following the Lord:

1. He knows the best path for us.

    Only God the Father, Jesus Christ His Son, and the Holy Spirit knows us because they live in us.

2. Jesus knows the danger.

    There are things we cannot see.

The Father who is our guide knows all the bears out there, He sees way ahead of us.

We don't know what is going to happen in the next minute.

He is all Omniscience.

He knows all things. There's know one out there that can guide you with everything, Only God.

Your friends can't tell you where to go, because they aren't you, they do not know how you feel inside. Only God knows, because our almighty God knows everything about you.

We are all vulnerable, that's why we need Almighty God so much.

Parents should tell their children, starting at a very young age, to trust in God, and that He is and will be always with them.

The reason God gives you trials and fires in your life because He has a purpose for it, its part of the plan.

There are places in your life when you look around and it doesn't seem good, trust in the Lord and follow Him.

I will say, "God show me exactly what to do at this point. Father, I am trusting you to guide me and tell me what to do.

He will be there and tell me because He is trustworthy at all times.

He will never let you give up. He will tell you to surrender to Him. I will surrender in His awesome victory, because I am trusting in God who created me.

God knows exactly where we are and how to get us home.

Our Responsibilities are:

Follow the guide and obey the guide.

Friends cannot tell you what to do because they don't know your strength and personality and definitely don't know your life.

If you ask your friend "What would God have me do in this situation?" They can't tell you, don't follow them or listen to them.

Sometimes we act like a mule. God speaks to us and we don't listen.

We want to take a path that looks good to us.

Make sure you let God be your guide because He knows.

Christ our pilot—He's got His hand on your shoulder when you go through stormy times. He not only guide you and get you through, His hand will be on your shoulder.

It starts by you acknowledging that you have lived your life without letting Jesus guide you.

Ask the Lord Jesus to forgive you for your sins, for being disobedient in not trusting Him to guide you.

Jesus died for all our sins. He paid the price for our eternal life. All we have to do is trust and have faith in Him.

The Father judged Him for our sins.

Say these words:
I will receive you for my savior.

And the moment you listen to Him, He will give you life at its best.

Ask by faith and trust in Him.

When His children cry to Him, He do not look the other way, He hears them.

Bible Study # 70
From the teaching of Rev Vernon King
Input also by Anita Cameron
Bible: King James Version

Faith In Life's Fires

During our lifetime we all must recognize who has the power, who knows everything coming and going, and who is always present.

We also must realize that God knows our future in advance.

Yes! He gives us a will to make decisions, but if you accept The Lord Jesus as your Lord and Savior then you will receive the Holy Spirit to guide you.

Sometime things don't seem to come out the way we want them to, but those that wait on the Lord and have faith will see that God has better things for them.

And when they look back and see what they wanted compared to what God has given them, they see what God gave them is much better and no one can take it away from them.

Therefore, faith and trust in God is your key to not being burned or singed.

The Book of Daniel Chapter 3

King Nebuchadnezzar made a decree that every man that hear the sound of the cornet, flute, harp, sachbut, psaltery, and all kinds of music must fall down and worship the golden image that he had set up. Anyone who didn't fall and worship the image would be cast into the midst of the burning fiery furnace.

There were three Hebrew men working for the king named Shad-rach, Me—shach and A-bed-ne-go that refused to fall down and worship the King's golden image he had set up. For they only bowled down and worship God, not a piece of wood with coverings of stone and mortar.

When the King was informed that they wouldn't fall down and worship the golden image he set up, he called them and confronted them, telling them that if they didn't worship his golden image he would have them cast in the midst of the burning fiery furnace.

He also said, "Who is that God that shall deliver you out of my hands?"

Daniel 3: 16
Shadrach, Meshach and Abednego, answered and said to the King, O Nebuchadnezzar, we are not careful to answer you in this matter.

Daniel 3: 17
If it be so, our God whom we serve is able to deliver us from the burning fiery furnace, and He will deliver us out of your hand, O king.

Daniel 3: 18
But if not, be it known unto you, O King that we will not serve your gods, nor worship the golden image, which you have set up.

Daniel 3: 21
The King had the three Hebrew men bound in their coats, their hose, and their hats and other garments, and was cast into the midst of the fiery furnace.

Because the King had commanded the furnace to be exceedingly hot, the men that cast Shadrach, Meshach and Abednego into the furnace died from the flames.

Yet Shadrach, Meshach and Abednego were standing in the midst of the fire talking to a fourth person.

Daniel 3: 24
Then Nebuchadnezzar the King was astonish, and rose up in haste and spoke, and said unto his counselors, "Did not we cast three men bound into the midst of the fire?"

They answered and said yes unto the king.

Daniel 3: 25
The King answered and said, "I see four men loose, walking in the midst of the fire, and they have no hurt, and the form of the fourth is like the Son of God.

And when the King called Shadrach, Meshach and Abednego to come out of the furnace, everyone saw that these three men, upon whose bodies the fire had no power. Nor was a hair on their head singed, neither were their coats change, and there was no smell of fire on them.

Daniel 3: 28
Then Nebuchadnezzar spoke, and said, "Blessed be the God of Shadrach, Meshach and Abednego. Who has sent His Angel and delivered His servants that trusted in Him, and have changed the king's word, and yielded their bodies that they might not serve nor worship any god, except their own God."

Daniel 3: 29
The King said, "Therefore I make a decree, that every people, nation and language which speak anything a miss against the God of Shadrach, Meshach and Abednego, shall be cut to pieces. Their houses shall be made a dunghill; because there is no other God that can deliver after this sort.

Daniel 3: 30
Then the king promoted Shadrach, Meshach and Abednego to even higher positions in the province of Babylon.

No matter how hot your fires are, if you have faith and trust in God, you will know He's right there with you. He knows all the answers and He will not let you singe or feel the heat.

Some people give up and go against God's commandments. They start stealing and conniving against people. They often say, "My back is up against the wall, and I have to do what I have to do to survive."

The more they involve themselves in themselves, the more they forget about God and Christ, their maker, provider and the only one with unconditional love for them.

Fires that we go through are challenges, and they do hurt terribly, but, we have a Father and a Lord and Savior Jesus who is always present Jehovah Shammah.

Those who trust and have faith and wait on the Lord will renew their strength and will mount with wings of an eagle and will run and not be weary and walk and not faint.

Bible Study # 71
From the teaching of Dr. Charles Stanley
Input also by Anita Cameron
Bible: King James Bible

Release From The Bondage of Rejection

A lot of people are living in bondage and aren't even aware of it.

If you live with something long enough you began to accept it.

If you are in bondage, it hurts more than you are willing to admit.

To accept your bondage will cause you to believe a lie and that is not the truth.

When people say derogatory things about you, you will believe what they say.

When people are rejected they sometime take it, as if they are unworthy.

It is a difference between accepting a person's conduct and accepting the person.

You might reject a person's conduct but still accept the person because rejection is very painful.

No one wants to feel rejected by anyone.

Romans 15:7
Wherefore receive you one another as Christ also received us to the glory of God.

Rejection is refusing to accept something.

A lot of parents cause their children to feel rejected at a young age and it stays with them.

When a person feels rejected they will act. Most feel like they are not wanted and they will take the rejection and dump it on their spouse or other people.

Some people demonstrate self-rejection; before they believe they are good enough, they must to be accepted by certain people.

Rejection Syndrome

1. A critical spirit: Criticizing themselves all the time.
2. Feel inferior.
3. Go beyond to get attention.
   Something inside of them controls them.
4. Perfectionism; they will procrastinate for fear of being rejected.
5. Anger and bitterness: They are quick to fly off the handle.
6. Easily hurt: They will feel less—than, when someone says something nice about them. Instead of feeling good about it, they will feel that the person is trying to interject something else.
7. A loner because they push people away from them.

Rejection is a very powerful tool of manipulation. Some people will use that to take advantage of others. When a person senses a needy person, they will try to get something they want from them.

How you deal with it?

God does not want us to have a rejection spirit.

You don't have to live that kind of life.

What causes rejection?

1. Growing up in a home where they were rejected by parents.

We must differentiate between rejections of the conduct not of the person.

2. Divorce.

> The worst thing a person can do is get involve with someone else without giving himself or herself time.

How do you get out of it?

You must develop a strong healthy feeling about yourself. Every single believer is a member of the family of God.

Colossians 1: 19
For it pleased the Father that in Him should all fullness dwell.

Colossians 1: 20
And, having made peace through the blood of His cross, by Him reconcile all things unto Himself; by Him, I say, whether they be things in earth, or things in heaven.

Colossians 1: 21
And you, that were sometimes alienated and enemies in your mind by wicked works, yet now have He reconciled.

Colossians 1: 22
In the body of His flesh through death, to present you holy and unblameable and unreproveable in His sight.

The basic of our feeling accepted is the atoning death of Jesus Christ.

Romans 8: 15
And having spoiled principalities and powers, He made a show of them openly, triumphing over them in it.

Romans 8: 16
Let know man judge you in meat (what you eat), or in drink, or in respect of a holy day, or of the new moon, or of the Sabbath days:

Romans 8: 17
Which are a shadow of things to come, but the body is of Christ.

You belong to God, and He's living through you.

Romans 5:5
And hope make not ashamed; because the love of God is shed abroad in our hearts by the Holy Ghost, which is given unto us.

Romans 5: 6
For when we were yet without strength in due time Christ died for you ungodly.

Romans 5: 7
For scarcely for a righteous man will one die: yet peradventure for a good man some would even dare to.

Romans 5: 8
But God commended His love towards us, in that while we were yet sinner Christ died for us.

We must keep in our heart and say "God saved me, I belong to God, and I am good."

God said this is your sense of worthiness, I sent my Son to die for you.

You are worthy because Christ died for you.

When someone rejects you say, "I am a child of God."

Romans 8: 11
But if the Spirit of Him that raised up Jesus from the dead dwell in you, He that raised up Christ from the dead shall also quicken your mortal bodies by His Spirit that dwell in you.

You are complete because the Holy Spirit dwells in you.

Jesus said I am coming to you through the power of the Holy Spirit.

Because we all belong to the almighty God and the Holy Spirit lives in us, how can we feel rejected. And what matter is it that someone rejects you.

God loves us unconditionally.
God forgives us completely.
God accepts us totally.
You are a whole person in Christ.

How can a person get out of this bondage?

God gave us a mind and a subconscious-mind. The Holy Spirit of God takes truth and is working in our hearts all night long.

Therefore, when you go to bed at night say, "God loves me unconditionally, completely and totally, and I am a whole person."

Feelings will follow the truth.

Jesus is our good Shepherd. He watches over us and provides for us.

Bible Study # 72
From the teachings of Dr. Charles Stanley
Input also by Anita Cameron and
Bible: New Beginner Bible (NBB)

It's Good To Give Thanks To God

When we pray we are often self-centered. Meaning, we pray for family and ourselves.

Often we start off by saying Lord please bless this one and that one and help me achieve this and that.

We forget to thank God for everything. Without God there would be nothing.

Psalm 92: 1
It is good to give thanks to the Lord, to sing praises to the Most High.

Psalm 92: 2
It is good to proclaim your unfailing love in the morning, your faithfulness in the evening.

Psalm 92: 3
Accompanied by the harp and lute and the harmony of the lyre.

Psalm 92: 4
You thrill me, Lord, with all you have done for me! I sing for joy because of what you have done.

Psalm 92: 5
O Lord, what great miracles you do! And how deep are your thoughts.

Giving gratitude to God for all His works.

We should give thanks to Him in the morning and thanks to Him in the evening.

He created us, guides us, and provides for us.

We are to teach our children from generation to generation the goodness of God and what He has done for us. We should teach our children to thank Him always for everything.

Psalm 50: 23
The Lord said, "But giving thanks is a sacrifice that truly honors me, If you keep to my path, I will reveal to you the salvation of God."

Psalm 105: 1
Give thanks to the Lord and proclaim His greatness. Let the whole world know what He has done.

Psalm 105: 2
Sing to Him; yes, sing His praises. Tell everyone about His miracles.

Psalm 106: 1
Praise the Lord! Give thanks to the Lord, for He is good! His faithful love endures forever.

Psalm 106: 2
Who can list the glorious miracles of the Lord? Who can ever praise Him half enough?

Psalm 107: 1
Give thanks to the Lord, for He is good! His faithful love endures forever.

Psalm 107: 2
Has the Lord redeemed you? Then speak out! Tell others He has saved you from your enemies.

God wants us to be thankful people. He has done so much for us, yet we take it for granted.

Reasons to give thanks

1. It Honors God.
   It's an act of obedience.

2. It Refocuses Our Attentions.
   It shows how grateful we are.

3. It Releases us from Anxiety.

   Philippians 4: 6
   Don't worry about anything, instead, pray about everything. Tell God what you need, and thank Him for all He has done.

   Philippians 4: 7
   If you do this, you will experience God's peace, which is far more wonderful than the human mind can understand. His peace will guard your heart and mind as you live in Christ Jesus.

   Are your circumstances higher than or greater than God?
   No, they are not.

   Thank God for the future, for what you are asking Him for in advance.

   Focus on the one that died for you.

4. Refreshes Our Relationship with Him.

   When you thank Him, you refresh your spirit. Something happens to you, spiritually and emotionally.

   He wants to pour out to us.

5. Reinforce Our Faith.

   God never changes. He is going to keep His word every time.

6. It Caused Our Spirit to Rejoice.

   Great is our faithfulness. If you praise God and thank Him before you get out of bed, He will get your body working.

How to Praise God

1. Verbally—Saying, God thank you so very much.

   God causes all things to work for good to those who love Him.

   There's Power in the name of Jesus. The bible says there's no name more powerful. He is ready, willing and able to help you.

2. Singing—God loves music to give Him thanks.
3. Live a godly life.
   Don't live in willing known sin. Action of obedience and the thoughts of obedience, and walking in obedience to Him, will be pleasing to the heart of God.

   If I live an obedient life, I am grateful to what He's done.

   When you confess your sins, He forgives you.

4. Give of yourself in public worship.
   God's primary reason for us to go to Church is to worship and praise Him. When you go to church and sing and praise Him God opens your heart to receive.

   Public Worshipping is very important, He wants us to assemble together and praise Him.

   It's funny how when we have something, we don't really express our gratitude until it's gone.

5. Give Generously. Tithe and offerings.

   All the things we have, God gives us. There' no excuse for not giving God. Whatever you give, will come back to you in some way.

   It has to do with our personal relationship with God to show our gratitude.

   You can't out give God.

Bible Study # 73
From the teachings of Dr. Charles Stanley
Input also by Anita Cameron
Bible: King James Version (KJV)

"Controlling Your Thoughts"

Our actions are the way we think, and our mind is utterly corrupted.

Romans 8: 5
For they that are after the flesh do mind the things of the flesh; but they that are after the Spirit the things of the Spirit.

Romans 8: 6
For the carnally minded is death; but to be spiritually minded is life and peace.

Romans 8: 7
Because the carnal mind is enmity against God; for it is not subject to the law of God, neither indeed can be.

Romans 1: 28
And even as they did not like to retain God in their knowledge, God gave them over to reprobate mind, to do those things, which are not convenient.

2nd Corinthians 11: 2
Paul said, he is speaking of a church, "For I am jealous over you with godly jealousy: For I have espoused you to one husband that I may present you as a chaste virgin to Christ."

2nd Corinthians 11: 3
We are warned of our mind for I fear lest by any means, as the serpent beguiled Eve through His subtility, so your minds should be corrupted from the simplicity that is in Christ.

2nd Corinthians 10: 4
For the weapon of our warfare are not carnal, but mighty through God to the pulling down of strong hold;

Our faith and trust in God should be strong.

Satan has a strong hold in your life, whereas he knows where he can get you. He observes you and sees what affects you and he tries to put things in your mind.

He can't read your mind, but he always tries to bring things up to your memory only to make you destroy yourself or someone else.

We can control our thinking.

When you trust your life to Jesus Christ, you become a child of God.

When your trust your life to Jesus Christ, you are identified with Him. Jesus sent the Holy Spirit to enable us.

Bible Study # 74
From the teaching of Dr. Charles Stanley,
Input also by Anita Cameron. Bibles: (KJV),
King James version. (NIV) New International
Version, and (NBB) New Beginners Bible

"God's Call to Genuine Repentance"

Repentance is a heart felt sorrow for sin. It is a commitment to forsake sin and be obedient by walking away from it.

A friend says to you, "I am a Christian." But they are still living in sin. They confess their sin to the Lord, yet they do it again and confess and do the sin over and over.

What's wrong with the friend? He or she has not made a change in their life. Therefore, there's no genuine repentance.

How important is repentance? A call to repentance is Salvation.

Matthew 3: 1-2
John the Baptist, preaching in the wilderness of Judaea, saying, repent everyone: for the Kingdom of Heaven is at hand.

Matthew 4: 17
From the time that Jesus began to preach, and say. Repent: for the Kingdom of God is at hand.

Repentance is a change in your life. You don't do the things you use to do, and be around certain people you use to associate with.

Luke 5: 36
Jesus said, "I came not to call the righteous, but sinners to repentance.

NIV Romans 2: 4
Do you show contempt for the riches of His kindness, tolerance and patience, not realizing that God's kindness leads you toward repentance?

NIV 2nd Peter 3: 9
The Lord is not slack concerning His promise, as some men count slackness; but is long suffering toward us, not willing that any should perish, but that all should come to repentance.

2nd Chronicles 7: 14
The Lord said, "If people, which are called by my name, shall humble themselves, and pray, and seek my face and turn from their wicked ways, then will I hear from heaven, and will forgive their sins, and will heal their land.

We live in an age where we tolerate sin. But God loves us too much to let us get by with it. Because He knows what happens to sinners.

Isaiah 55: 6
Seek the Lord while He may be found, call upon Him while He is near.

Isaiah 55: 7
Let the wicked forsake His way, and the unrighteous man His thoughts: and let Him return unto the Lord, and He will have mercy upon Him; and to our God, for He will abundantly pardon.

There is no genuine repentance, unless they turn their life around.

Repentance is heart-felt.

To change you have to have the power of the Holy Spirit in your life.

The message of repentance must be taught all over the world.

NBB Luke 15:11-24
The story of the Lost Son

Jesus said, "A man had two sons, the younger son told his father, "I want my share of your estate now, instead of waiting until you die." So his father agreed to divide his wealth between his sons.

A few days later his younger son packed all his belongings and took a trip to a distant land, and there he wasted all his money on wild living.

About the time his money ran out, a great famine swept over the land, and he began to starve. He persuaded a local farmer to hire him to feed his pigs. The boy became so hungry that even the pods he was feeding the pigs looked good to him. But no one gave him anything.

When he finally came to his senses, he said to himself, "At home even the hired men have food enough to spare, and here I am, dying of hunger! I will go home to my father and say "Father, I have sinned against both heaven and you, and I am no longer worthy of being called your son. Please take me on as a hired man."

So he returned home to his father. And while he was still a long distance away his father saw him coming. Filled with love and compassion, he ran to his son, embraced him and kissed him.

His son said to him, "father I have sinned against both heaven and you, and I am no longer worthy of being called your son.

But his father said to the servants, "Quick! Bring the finest robe in the house and put it on him. Get a ring for his finger and sandals for his feet. And kill the calf we have been fattening in the pen. We must celebrate with a feast.

For this son of mine was dead and has now returned to life. He was lost, but now he is found.

As you can see the son came to his senses, he left his old style of living in sin. What really got his attention is that he lost everything.

The same way his father accepted him back with open arms, is the same way our Father in heaven will accept us.

How many times do we remember to repent when things aren't going well for us?

If you can't straighten up your life, God will change, when you respond a genuine sorrow for your sin.

Something has to take place in a person's life.

a. Change of conduct.
b. Change of way of thinking.
c. Change in their conversation.
d. Change in their character.

John 3: 16
For God so loved the world that He gave His only begotten Son, so that everyone who believes in Him will not perish but have eternal life.

Romans 10: 9
For If you confess with your mouth that Jesus is lord and believe in your heart that God raised Him from the dead, you will be saved.

Romans 10: 10
For it is by believing in your heart that you are made right with God, and it is by confessing with your mouth that you are save.

Romans 10: 11
Anyone who believes in Him will not be disappointed.

Romans 10: 13
For anyone who calls on the name of the Lord will be saved."

To believe in Jesus involves and includes repentance.

Repentance—A person has a sorrow for what he or she has done.

When that person means it, the Holy Spirit will abide in him or her and the Spirit of God lives in them.

For a person that wants to be saved, must acknowledge they've sinned before God.

Matthew 7: 21
Jesus said, "Not all people who sound religious are really godly. They may refer to me as Lord, but they still won't enter the Kingdom of Heaven. The decisive issue is whether they obey my Father in heaven.

Matthew 7: 22
On judgment day many will tell me, "Lord, Lord, we prophesied in your name and cast out demons in your name and performed many miracles in your name."

Matthew 7: 23
But I will reply, "I never knew you. Go away; the things you did were unauthorized."

When we confess our sins we must repent.

The reason it would not be a genuine repentance is because we didn't let the sin go.

I am willing to walk away, because God does not want it in my life.

When I genuinely repent from my sin, I will no longer feel free to do it. My conscience will not let me.

The Holy Spirit's responsibility is to convict you for your sin by revealing what is right and wrong.

Proverbs 28: 13
People who cover over their sins will not prosper. But if they confess and forsake them, they will receive mercy.

The Lord loves us too much to let us wreck and ruin our life.

Bible Study # 75
Bible study by Anita Cameron
Bible: KJV-King James Version

"A Realtor For The Lord"

Jesus said, "In my Father's house there are many mansions, I go to prepare a place for you.

When Jesus died for us to take away our sins, He set us free. We are free from bondage and we are redeemed.

But, many people have not accepted Jesus as their Lord and Savior.

Some people have not been taught about Jesus and some don't trust ministers (preachers) to teach them.

Most people don't read the bible and some of those that do read need help in understanding what they are reading.

Satan is always lurking trying to steal, kill, and destroy. Many times Satan tares people away from the truth.

Satan does this by either using someone else to deter them, or knowing the person's weaknesses, builds on that by constantly reminding them of their past and repeatedly try to confirm their weaknesses.

We as Christians, saved by grace, must deter people from Satan and bring them to peace, love, grace and harmony.

We must become Realtors for the Lord; by bringing people to the New Garden of Eden. There's no cost; it's theirs for the asking.

To Be A Realtor for the Lord

1. You must believe in Jesus and that He came to earth, born of a virgin, died being incorruptible, taking away the sins of the earth, went to hell and got the key of life, was resurrected, and gave all who believe in Him eternal life.
2. You must believe that even though we all fall short, being tempted and committing sins, but, know that if you ask Jesus for forgiveness of your sin in sincerity, He will wipe it out, no more to be remembered.

Psalm 103: 10
The Lord has not dealt with us after our sins; nor rewarded us according to our iniquities.

Psalm 103: 11
For as the heaven is high above the earth, so great is His mercy towards them that fear Him.

Psalm 103: 12
As far as the east is from the west, so far has He removed our transgressions from us.

Psalm 103: 13
Like a father that pities His children so the Lord pities them that fear Him.

You are the only one who keeps bring up in your memory your past sins. Satan will constantly remind you of your sins, to deter you from your beliefs. Most of the time you don't have enough faith and belief in God's word therefore you give Satan and opening.

You must read and believe His words. His word gives you the ability to live in peace, love, and harmony.

3. You must have faith and trust in Jesus.

Hebrew 11: 1
Now faith is the substance of things hoped for, the evidence of things not seen.

Galatians 2:20
I am crucified with Christ; nevertheless I live; yet not I, but live in me, and the life which I now live in the flesh, I live by the faith of the Son of God, who love me and gave Himself for me.

You must have faith, knowing that all power is in His hand and He knows everything.

He knows our past and our future. That's why we leave everything in His hand, and pray to Him for guidance when making decisions.

4. We must have charity (love). We are not to always consider our family and ourselves only. We are not to look down on people who are not as fortunate as we are. We must enlighten ourselves in knowing that we are all God's children, and that He loves us all.
5. We must forgive. When we feel someone has done something wrong to us, and we must pray to the Lord to help that person to become a better person. It doesn't mean you have to be around that person, but when we forgive, we set our soul free.
6. As a Realtor you will bring souls to the Kingdom of heaven. Where everlasting life is and where the new heaven and earth is.

Isaiah 67: 17
Jesus said, "For, behold I create a new heaven and new earth: and the former shall not be remembered, nor come into mind.

Revelation 21: 1
John said, "and I saw a new heaven and a new earth: For the first heaven and the first earth passed away: and there was no more sea.

Revelation 21: 2
And I John saw the holy city, New Jerusalem, coming down from God out of heaven, prepared as a bride adorned for her husband.

Revelation 21: 3
And I heard a great voice out of heaven saying, behold, the tabernacle of God is with men, and He will dwell with them, and they shall be His people, and God Himself shall be their God.

Revelation 21: 4
And God shall wipe away all tears from their eyes; and there shall be no more death, neither sorrow, nor crying, neither shall there be any more pain. For the former things are passed away.

Revelation 21: 6
And He said unto me, "It is done. I am Alpha and Omega, the beginning and the end. I will give unto him that is thirsty of the fountain of the water of life freely.

Revelation 21: 7
He that overcomes shall inherit all things; and I will be His God, and he shall be my son."

Revelation 21: 8
For the Lord said, "But the fearful, and unbelieving, and the abominable, and murders, whoremongers, sorcerers, idolaters, and all liars, shall have their part in the lake which burn with fire and brimstone which is the second death.

You don't want to be in that number nor do you want anyone else to be there.

8. As a Realtor you will be a testimony of what God has done for you and there's nothing impossible for Him to do. What He has done for you, you know He can do for others.
9. As a Realtor you must practice what you teach or preach. Your message should come from the word (Bible), not what you feel people want to hear.
10. As a Realtor you must have integrity; not boasting because of what you know, but being humble and grateful to God for the knowledge and wisdom He's given you to share with others.
11. As a Realtor for the Lord you will be the cause of many people going to their new home, the New Garden of Eden.

Table of Contents

1. When God is Silent 307
2. Letting God handle the burden of your life 311
3. Divine Intervention 316
4. Landmine of Unforgiveness 323
5. Divine Nature of God Inside of You 327
6. Understanding Our Divinity 332
7. When your Fire Goes out 335
8. The Power of the Blood 339
9. Protecting your Future 343
10. Our God of Grace 347
11. Hell Is Real 354
12. The Truth Is Salvation 358
13. Dealing with False Teaching 362
14. Can God use you 367
15. Revelation of Royalty 371

Bible Study # 76
From the teaching of Dr. Charles Stanley
Input also by Anita Cameron,
Bible NBB—New Beginners Bible

"When God Is Silent"

Have you ever felt that God is giving you the silent treatment?

You are praying and asking God for something and you feel nothings happening.

Do you believe He's not listening?

God sometimes is silent and He has a purpose for it.

John 11: 1-15
This is a story in the bible about a man named Lazarus who was very sick. He lived with his two sisters Mary and Martha. The two sisters sent a message to Jesus telling Him that Lazarus was sick. Jesus was very close to them. He loved them the way He loves us. His sisters wanted Jesus to come and heal him.

When Jesus received the message, He said, "Lazarus's sickness will not end in death. No it is for the glory of God." Even though He loved Martha, Mary, and Lazarus, He stayed where He was for the next two days and did not go to them.

Finally He said to His disciples, "let's go Judea again. Our friend Lazarus has fallen asleep, but now I will go and wake him up.

His disciples said, "Lord if he is sleeping that means he is getting better. They thought Jesus meant Lazarus was having a good night's sleep.

They had no idea that Lazarus was dead. But Jesus knew.

Then Jesus told them plainly, "Lazarus is dead. And for your sake, I am glad I wasn't there, because this will give you another opportunity to believe in me;

When Jesus got there Lazarus was already buried. He was in a cave wrapped in cloth with a stone rolled in front of it.

Jesus raised Lazarus from the dead.

This is a good example of why He was silent, so that not only His disciples, but that the whole town would believe in Him, and that He is the Son of God, sent by Him.

When you pray and nothing happens, have you ever been angry with God?

Most of us do when we can't have our way.

Some of us might not feel angry, but want to ask Him why.

I want you to see that His silent is very, very good.

Sometimes He appears silent and we shut Him out.

Keep in your heart that sometimes He's silent:

1. To get our attention.
2. Sin that is not confessed.
3. We are not ready to listen to Him. Especially if there's something He doesn't want us to have.

Remember Satan will come to manipulate you to think a certain way.

4. He teaches us to trust in Him.

When He's silent, it doesn't mean He's not listening.

Silence is His way of having us trust in Him.

5. He wants us to be able to distinguish between His voice and other voices.

He is always teaching us something.

When you feel like a wall is between you and God, keep on praying and trust in Him.

We are not to quit because He's silent.

He's working on it, and there is a reason for it. *It's always for our good.*

When you don't have a need at all, do you have quiet time with Him? Or is the only time you want to hear from Him is when you are in need?

What God wants us to have is an intimate relationship with Him.

Can you trust God just being in His presents?

How do we respond to God's silence?

Everyone responds differently, but most of us respond by being:

1. Disappointed.
2. Discouraged.

Don't stop praying because He's silent. It doesn't mean He's not listening.

3. Confused.
4. Have Doubt.
5. Guilt. Feeling God must be disgusted with us, or we'll feel something's wrong.
6. Angry.
7. Feeling separated from God.
8. Fear.

How should we respond when God is silent?

Silent is not always bad. He's being good to you. He's getting our attention, because He wants us to have an intimate relationship with Him. He wants us to obey, trust, love and have faith in Him, simply because He is God.

1. Ask God *why*. We have a right to ask God why.
2. Remember His silence does not mean that He's inactive.
3. Quietly Trust Him.

He will perfect what is in our life.

Psalm 46: 10
"Be silent and know that I am God! I will be honored by every nation.
I will be honored throughout the world."

4. Anticipate a more intimate relationship with Him.
5. Respect the right of God to be silent.
6. Read God's word.

Start reading His word anywhere in the Bible. Start reading Psalms.

When you do read the Bible the Holy Spirit interprets things to your heart.

Keep praying and reading His words. Your break through comes by you continuing to pray and read his word.

Intimacy is that we are one. We should teach our children at a very young age, which would help our children with their early life.

If you are not a believer, ask God to forgive you.

If you are a believer, get on your knees and pray to Him.

Everyone should get on His or her knees to pray to God. For He is almighty, knows everything from beginning to end, and has all power to do all things.

If you will practice silence before Him, all of those things, sickness, problems with money and marriages will pass away.

He's going to give you a sense of Himself.

Bible Study # 77
From the teaching of Dr. Charles Stanley,
Input also by Anita Cameron,
Bible: King James Version (KJV)

"Letting God Handle The Burdens In Your Life"

Why is it that some people can go through a lot of hardship and pain and still keep a smile on their face?

Yet there are others who by looking at them you can tell they are burdened down.

When you have burdens in your life, the pain might not show outwardly, but inwardly you're all bent over.

Does God set a limit on our burdens?

Yes! God knows our limit, and God does not let us take on no more than we can bear.

We want to rid ourselves of all burdens, but sometimes these burdens are God given, and sometimes we cause them ourselves.

When we burden ourselves we are emotionally and spiritually bent over on the inside.

Because of some things you have done in the past can cause you to feel a lot of guilt.

Burden of guilt is the worst burden to carry.

Matthew 11: 28
Jesus said, "Come unto me, all you that labor and are heavy laden, and I will give you rest.

Matthew 11: 29
Take my yoke upon you and learn of me; for I am meek and lowly in heart: and you shall find rest unto your souls.

Matthew 11: 30
For my yoke is easy, and my burden is light."

Burdens are heaviness on the spirit, soul and mind. It weighs you down.

A God given burden is a divine communication.

For example in The Old testament God gave His prophets messages. The Prophets felt the burden of delivering the word of God to the people.

How God places burdens on our hearts today, is that you feel this very strong desire to witness to someone, or you feel very strongly about praying for someone or giving to someone.

That is one way God gives us direction.

God lays burdens on our hearts by directing us, getting our attention and they are not all bad.

Psalm 38: 4
For mine iniquities are gone over mine head: as a heavy burden they are too heavy for me.

When a person lives with guilt it is destructive, because you cannot live with a burden of guilt.

Even if you have a sense of guilt you are burdened.

Now there are some people who have burdens we cannot imagine.

For example: A child having to live with fatal a disease all their life.

We have know idea how blessed we are.

How Do We Handle These Burdens in Our Life

1. God's invitation is all-inclusive.

   Matthew 11: 28,
   Jesus said, "Come unto me, all you that labor and are heavy laden, and I will give you rest."

   If you've never trusted Jesus in your life it is a burden, because you will not know of His promises.

   1st John 2: 1
   My little children, these things I write unto you, that you sin not. And if any man sin, we have an advocate with the Father, Jesus Christ the righteous.

   If you are not a believer and you become a believer, He automatically takes away your sins.

2. God's invitation is motivated by love.

   He does not want us in bondage with anything or anyone.

   He wants it so that you never have to fear coming to Him.

   He loves us know matter what.

   Psalm 55: 22
   Cast your burdens upon the Lord and He shall sustain you. He shall never suffer the righteous to be moved.

   Psalm 68: 19
   Blessed be the Lord, who daily loaded us with benefits, even the God of our salvation.

   If He bears it, I don't have to bear it. He helps me daily.

Everybody's got something to deal with in life. Maybe financial problems, drug problems, marriage break-up, or just somebody did something to them.

Praise is to God to the person that can say, I am able to live in the mist of it, and talk about it and feel all right because I am motivated by love.

3. God's invitation is encouraging.

God handles the burdens in your life:

1. If you come to Him and lay it down.

    Sometimes we don't come to Him and discuss it with Him. We don't deal with it by trusting in the Lord and having faith that He will take care of us and carry our burden.

2. If you follow His instructions.

    He has never failed to keep His promises.

3. Surrender your will to God.

    If you get under the yoke with Him, He will carry the burden.

    He takes the weigh off us, and then we began to walk in His way, and think the way He thinks.

    Coming into a relationship with Him is a submission to Him.

    He will take the weigh away, and He will lift the burden away.

    I don't have to be bent over with burdens.

    There's a multitude of people that are having a civil war within themselves. They will not go the Lord, or they just don't trust and have faith in Him to carry their burdens for them.

    God wants to carry your weigh. But first you have to come to Him.

God will equip you to face any circumstance in your life. It begins with surrender.

4. Learn From God.

   Learn about Him. God wants you to come to Him in prayer. Surrender to Him, don't try to lie or cover up, because He knows everything about you.

   He doesn't take your burden without taking you.

   The burden could be there, but He takes the weigh off.

5. Trust God.

   Spirit, soul, mind and body has to be surrendered to Him.

   Proverbs 3: 5
   Trust in the Lord with all your heart; and lean not unto your own understanding.

   Proverbs 3: 6
   In all your ways acknowledge Him, and He shall direct your path.

6. Leave your burden with God.

   Because of who He is, Because of His power, and because of His promises.

   Ask yourself, what is this thing that's burden me?

   I will bring it to Him and I will trust Him.

   One thing for sure you don't have to beg.

   Jesus said, "Why carry something so heavy when my way is right and my way is easy.

   That burden can be removed if you submit yourself to the Lord asking Him to save you from your sins right now.

   If you are a believer, you don't have to carry burdens.

Bible Study # 78
Bible Study by Anita Cameron
Bible: King James Version (KJV)

"Divine Intervention"

The Lord intervenes in our lives. He has given us a free will to choose, but every now and then He intervenes.

When the Lord intervenes, no one or nothing can stop it but you, and sometimes you can't stop it if it's His will.

You can let it be by His will or by your will.

The Lord Intervenes:

1. To protect you from the enemy.
2. To guide you towards a path He has planned for you.
3. To guide you away from something you will regret.
4. To protect you from yourself.
5. To fight your battles.
6. To keep you from sinning against Him.
7. To get your attention.
8. Because you believe in Him.
9. To show you, you can't hide from Him.

Sometimes we go through trials and tribulations because He's trying to get our attention.

Sometimes we put earthly things before Him. We do not put Him first, and keep in our hearts and mind that He made everything. His wisdom and knowledge is far more advanced than what we can imagine or comprehend.

We can save ourselves from worry, stress and feeling lost by going to the Lord in prayer and believing He knows all, sees all and have power over everything.

The Lord knows what's ahead of us and what's behind us. All we know is the right now. Two minutes from now could change our whole life, but He knows.

Therefore it is best and proven overtime, that if you are a believer of Jesus and that He died to set you free and saved you by grace and mercy that you are His child and you are guaranteed everlasting life.

In Geneses chapter 11

The Lord intervened when everyone spoke the same language and decided to build a city and tower whose top was to reach into heaven.

Geneses 11: 5
And the Lord came down to see the city and the tower, which the children of men built.

Geneses 11: 6
Ands the Lord said, "Behold, the people are one and they have all one language; and this they begin to do: and now nothing will be restrained from them, which they have imagined to do."

Geneses 11: 7
The Lord said, "Go to, let us go and there confound their language, that they may not understand one another's speech.

The Lord knew that they were heading towards something they would regret. And He was saving them from themselves.

In Geneses Chapter 12

Abraham was afraid that if he didn't say Sara was his sister the Egyptians would kill him, therefore Abraham deceived the Egyptians Pharaoh that Sara was his sister and not his wife also.

When Pharaoh took Sara into his house, the Lord intervened by plaguing Pharaoh's house

Geneses 12: 18
And Pharaoh called Abrams and said, "What is this that you have done unto me? Why did you not tell me that she was your wife?

Geneses 12: 19
Why did you say "She is my sister?" I might have taken her to be my wife. Now
Therefore take your wife and go.

In Geneses chapter 20

Again Abraham journeyed to another place and deceived Abimelech the king of Gerar that Sara was his sister and King Abimelech sent and took Sara.

Geneses 20: 3
But God came to Abimelech in a dream by night, and said to him, "Behold you art but a dead man, for the woman for which you have taken, for she is a man's wife.

Geneses 20:4
But Abimelech had not come near her: and he said Lord, will you slay also a righteous nation?

Genesis 20:5
Did he (talking about Abraham) not say unto me, she is my sister? And she even herself said, "he is my brother." In the integrity of my heart and innocence of my hand have I done this.

Geneses 20: 6
And God said unto him in a dream, yes, I know that you did this in the integrity of your heart; for I also withheld you from sinning against me; Therefore suffered I you not to touch her.

God not only intervened to save Sara, but He also intervened to save King Abimelech from sinning against Him.

How many times has God saved you from sinning against Him?

God intervened when Moses was born to a Hebrew mother and Pharaoh had made a decree that all Hebrew children age two and under would be killed. He feared the take over of his kingdom by them because of their population increase.

His sister raised Moses in Pharaoh's house as her child.

God had a plan for Moses and that was for him to lead the Hebrew people out of the land of Egypt.

When Moses was leading the Hebrew people out of Egypt, God intervened. He opened the Red Sea for them to pass through and closed it so that the Egyptian army could not pass through.

In Daniel Chapter 3

God intervened, when Shadrach, Meshach and Abednego was placed in the fiery furnace to die, because they would not bowl down before the golden image that the King had made. They only worshipped the Lord God.

Daniel 3: 24
Then King Nebuchadnezzar was astounded, and rose up in haste, and spoke, and said unto His counselors, "Did not we cast three men bound into the midst of the fire?" They answered and said unto the King, "yes."

Daniel 3: 25
He said, I see four men loose, walking in the midst of the fire, and they have no hurt; and the form of the fourth is like the Son of God.

God protected them from their enemy.

In Daniel Chapter 6

Daniel was placed in the Lion's den, because of jealousy. The king had signed a petition not knowing that it was a set up against Daniel to have him killed. So when Daniel was seen praying to God three times a day that was against what they had in the petition for the King to sign.

So when Daniel was placed in the lion's den, King Darius was very upset and couldn't sleep.

Daniel 6: 20
And when the King came to the den, he cried with lamentable voice unto Daniel: and the King spoke and said to Daniel, O Daniel servant of the living God, Is your God, whom you serve continually, able to deliver you from the lions?

At that time he had no idea that Daniel was still alive.

Daniel 6: 22
Then Daniel said unto the King, "My God has sent His angel and has shut the lion's mouths, that they have not hurt me: For I have been found innocent in His sight. And I have not wronged you, your majesty."

Daniel 6: 23
The King was overjoyed and ordered that Daniel be lifted from the den. Not a scratch was found on him because he had trusted in his God.

Because Daniel believed in God, he knew that He would provide. God intervened. He's JEHOVAH—JIREH.

Then there was Jonah who tried to run from God when the word of the Lord came to him to rise up and cry against Nineveh, Because God had seen how wicked its people were.

Jonah 1:3
Jonah rose up to flee unto another city call TarsHish, from the presence of the Lord. He got on a ship thinking he was getting away from the presence of the Lord.

Jonah 1: 4
But the Lord sent out a great wind into the sea, and there was a mighty tempest in the sea, so that the ship was like to be broken.

Everyone was afraid, but Jonah was fast asleep laying into the sides of the ship. The others on the ship said, "lets cast lots to find out who caused this evil upon us." When they cast the lots, the lot fell on Jonah.

Jonah 1: 9
Jonah said unto them, I am a Hebrew; and I fear the Lord, the God of heaven, which has made the sea and the dry land.

Jonah asked them to throw him overboard so that the sea would be calm. After a while they did throw Jonah into the sea and the sea became calm.

Jonah 1: 17
Now the Lord had prepared a great fish to swallow up Jonah and Jonah was in the belly of the fish three days and three nights.

Jonah 2: 1
Then Jonah prayed unto the Lord his God out of the fish's belly.

Jonah 2: 10
And the Lord spoke unto the fish, and it vomited Jonah upon the dry land.

God intervened. He got Jonah's attention, and He also guided Him towards the path He had planned for Him. And also showed Him, he could not hide from the Lord.

In Geneses Chapter 3,

After Adam's sin, The Lord God told Adam because you have sin.

Genesis 3: 19
In the sweat of your face shall you eat bread, (meaning he had to work for his food) until you return unto the ground; for out of it were you taken; for dust you are, and unto dust shall you return.

Before Jesus our Lord and Savior came down to earth, we all were destine to die and go back into the ground as dust never to be anymore.

Oh! But, Jesus' divine intervention,
He was there in the beginning with God, and all things were made by Him. He came and gave His life not only for you and me, but also for the whole world. He made the ultimate sacrifice so that all that believed in Him would have eternal life.

We are now spiritual beans, children of God, going through this earthly life heading to our home into paradise.

When Paul was known as Saul, he persecuted all the believers of Jesus. One day when he was going on a mission to gather and bound any man or woman that believed in Jesus and bring them to Jerusalem, Jesus' divine intervention stopped Paul and made Him one of his apostles.

Acts 9: 3
And as Saul journeyed, he came near Damascus and suddenly a brilliant light from heaven beamed down upon him!

Acts 9: 4
He fell to the ground and heard a voice saying to him, "Saul! Saul! Why are you persecuting me?"

He became blind and was sent to Damascus. When he got there his eyes were opened and he believed in Jesus and went throughout the countries preaching and praising Jesus. He had a testimony and a revelation to tell about Jesus.

Jesus changed his name from Saul to Paul.

I want you to sit down and meditate on how many times that you know that God has intervened in your life.

Then I want you to praise Him and thank Him.

I pray that by you reading this, you will have joy in your heart knowing that the Lord intervenes in your life, and that you will ask Him to continue to do so.

We are not perfect, and no one can take on this life by himself or herself.

Remember no one can take away what God has planned for you but you.

Seek the Holy Spirit to guide you.

Bible Study # 79
From the teaching of Dr. Charles Stanley,
Input also by Anita Cameron
Bible: New Beginners Bible (NBB) and
King James Version (KJV)

"Landmine of Unforgiveness"

Unforgiveness is the refusal to lay down resentment, anger and hostility.

We sometime do not forgive because of what we think or what we feel our friends may say or think.

Unforgiveness can and will imprison you.

What does Jesus say about this?

Ephesians 4: 26
Jesus said, "Don't sin by letting anger gain control over you. Don't let the sun go down while you are still angry."

Ephesians 4: 27
For anger gives a mighty foothold to the Devil.

Ephesians 4: 28
If you are a thief, stop stealing. Begin using your hands for honest works and then give generously to others in need.

Ephesians 4: 29
Don't use foul or abusive language. Let everything you say be good and helpful, so that your words will be an encouragement to those who hear them.

Ephesians 4: 30
And do not bring sorrow to God's Holy Spirit by the way you live. Remember, He is the one who has identified you as His own, guaranteeing that you will be saved on the day of redemption.

Ephesians 4: 31
Get rid of all bitterness, rage, anger, harsh words, and slander, as well as all types of malicious behavior.

Ephesians 4: 32
Instead, be kind to each other, tenderhearted, forgiving one another, just as God through Christ has forgiven you.

When we trusted Jesus to be our Lord and Savior we forfeited our way of being unforgiving.

We cannot defend an unforgiving spirit.

The same way God has forgiven us, He wants us to forgive others. We have to lay unforgiveness down, because it becomes an acid living inside of us.

Jesus is known for forgiveness, He forgives us for our sins past, present and future.

Unforgiveness is destructive and a form of bondage.

In a marriage or a relationship, when a person brings into the marriage or relationship things from the past that has hurt them or they felt that someone did them wrong, the marriage or relationship is defeated before it starts. Because that person has an unforgiving spirit in them, and they refuse to lay it down and they become self-centered.

A person with an unforgiving spirit has to deal with it. If they don't, they will continue to carry around old baggage, which will keep them in bondage.

Romans 12: 19
Never avenge yourselves. Leave that to God, for it is written, "I will take vengeance; I will repay those who deserve it, says the Lord.

There is no limit to how many times you are to forgive. Eventhough you might say to yourself, I have forgiven that person too many times, and I am not doing it anymore.

Matthew 18: 21
Peter came to the Lord and asked, "Lord how often should I forgive someone who sins against me Seven times?"

Matthew 18: 22
No! Jesus replied, "Seventy times seven!"

Consequence of people that is unforgiving:

1. It begins working on your spirit, heart and mind.

    It starts working on a person and you'll be able to see it in their conversation that it's working on their character and personality.

2. Affects the human body by creating tension and stress.

    It affects your heart and blood pressure.

    It causes diseases.

Jesus made us to live in joy and contentment. It may not be that way all the time, but there is a peace and joy in you when things are happening that you cannot explain.

   You find yourself saying, "This doesn't affect me."

3. Affects your prayer life.

    It is out of character for God to hear you praying about something and you can't forgive.

4. Affects your worship.

It cannot be well with your soul if you feel unforgiveness for someone.

    As your Father has forgiven you, you also must forgive that person that wronged you.

5. Affects your scripture reading.

How can you have understanding when reading the scripture and apply them to your life when you are unforgiving.

6. It short-circuits your faith.
7. Warps your perspectives of your life.

How do you deal with it?

1. Acknowledge your unforgiving spirit and identify the person.

    Confess to God and talk to Him about what the person's done.

2. Choose to no longer hold an unforgiving spirit towards that person.

    You say and feel, "As the Lord forgave me, I must forgive others."

    It doesn't mean you won't remember it. Forgetting in one thing, forgiving is another thing.

    I ask you to get out of those shackles and forgive. You will be able to say, "I am free at last."

    And you don't have to be around that person anymore. Or be in their presents anymore.

    When you trust the Lord Jesus as your Lord and Savior, you will ask Him to give you a forgiven spirit so that you can be free.

    Say, "I choose with the grace of God to lay down un-forgiveness. If it crops up again, I will lay it down again."

    I pray that the Holy Spirit will sink this in everyone's life for a new beginning.

Bible Study # 80
From teachings of Pastor Bill Winston
Input also by Anita Cameron.
Bible: King James Version (KJV), and
New Beginners Bible (NBB)

"Divine Nature of God Inside Of You"

It is God's plan for you to operate in the super natural.

You must have faith and read the Word. Let the Word be in your heart.

Anyone in Christ is a new creature.

Ephesians 5: 1
Be you therefore followers of God, as dear children.

Ephesians 5: 2
And walk in love, as Christ also loved us, and has given Himself for us an offering and a sacrifice to God for a sweet smelling savor.

We have the same nature as God. We are going to start acting like that.

Jesus our Lord and savior operated in the super natural.

Before Jesus had sent all the people away, He had His disciples get into the ship and go on the other side while He sent the multitude of people away.

Matthew 14: 23
And when Jesus had sent the multitude of people away, He went up into a mountain apart to pray: and when the evening was come, He was there alone.

Matthew 14: 24
But the ship was now in the midst of the sea, tossed with waves: for the wind was contrary.

Matthew 14: 25
About three o'clock in the morning Jesus came to them, walking on the water.

Matthew 14: 26
When the disciples saw Him, they screamed in terror, thinking He was a ghost.

Matthew 14: 27
But Jesus spoke to them at once. "It is all right," He said. "I am here! Don't be afraid.

Matthew 14: 28
Then Peter called to Him, "Lord, if it's really you, tell me to come to you by walking on water."

Matthew 14: 29
Jesus said, "all right come." So Peter went over the side of the boat and walked on the water toward Jesus.

Matthew 14: 30
But when he looked around at the high waves, he was terrified and began to sink. "Save me Lord" he shouted.

Matthew 14: 31
Instantly Jesus reached out His hand and grabbed Him. Jesus said, "You don't have much faith." "Why did you doubt me?"

How many people know that God is

Omnipotence—All Power
Omniscience—Knowing Everything
Omnipresent—Everywhere at all times

Another time after Jesus had sent the multitude of people away He calmed the storm.

Mark 4: 35
As the evening came, Jesus said to His disciples, "Let's cross to the other side of the lake."

Mark 4: 36
He was already in the boat, so they started out, leaving the crowds behind, although other small ships followed.

Mark 4: 37
But soon a fierce storm arose. High waves began to break into the boat until it was nearly full of water.

Mark 4: 38
Jesus was sleeping at the back of the boat with His head on a cushion. Frantically they woke Him up, shouting, "Teacher, don't you even care that we are going to drown?"

Mark 4: 39
When He woke up, He rebuked the wind and said to the water, "Quiet down!" suddenly the wind stopped, and there was a great calm.

Mark 4: 40
And Jesus asked them, "Why are you so afraid? Do you still not have faith in me?"

The Father is sending them out knowing a storm is coming.

What you can't see is a manifestation of what you can see.

You must have Faith.

Mark 4: 41
And the feared exceedingly said one to another, "What manner of man is this, that even the wind and the sea obey Him?"

What the enemy Satan tries to do is choke faith out of you.

He constantly tries to remind you of something you have done, so that fear can come into your heart.

Remember when you accepted Jesus as your Lord and Savior, all of your sins were forgiven. He paid the price for you, the whole world and me. So that who so ever believes in Him shall be free.

You are in the world, but you are not of the world. You are a new creature in Christ.

Revelations 12: 9
And the great dragon was cast out, that old serpent, called the Devil, and Satan, which deceived the whole world; he was cast out into the earth, and his angels were cast out with him.

Satan accuses you day and night.

Revelations 12: 10
And John said, "I heard a loud voice saying in heaven, now is come salvation, and strength, and the Kingdom of our God, and the power of His Christ. For the accuser of our brothers and sisters is cast down, which accused them before our God day and night.

Revelations 12: 11
And they overcame him by the blood of the Lamb, and by the word of their testimony; and they loved not their lives unto death.

Isaiah 54: 4
Fear not; you will no longer live in shame. The shame of your youth and the sorrows of widowhood will be remembered no more.

All the shame you have, all the shame the Devil tries to remind you of, Jesus took our sin, and our punishment away with His blood.

He was in heaven and came down to earth as the First man born of God. He went in Combat with Satan and took back all that Satan had taken from us including our dignity.

Up in heaven Jesus is our defender.

When Satan, the Devil accuses us, Jesus is our defender. He must have two witnesses. The first witness is His blood, and we are the second witness.

Therefore you have to keep your mind and heart open with the Word.

Don't listen to people, when they tell you, you are nothing and you'll never be anything. If you do you will feel condemned.

When you feel condemned you let sickness and diseases come into you.

2nd Corinthians 5: 17
Therefore if any man be in Christ, he is a new creature" Old things are passed away, behold, all things are become new.

2nd Corinthians 5: 21
For God has made Jesus to be a sin for us, who knew no sin: that we might be made the righteousness of God in Him.

Romans 8: 1
There is therefore now no condemnation to them, which are in Christ Jesus, who walk not after the flesh, but after the Spirit.

Righteousness is your nature.

Do you think anything was made without the Lord?

God's divine intervention gave man a divine nature of God, which enabled man to make things convenient for us to live in this world.

For instance: Cars, airplanes, telephones, consuming water and equipment to improve our daily life.

God has made life easier for us because He loves us and knows our existence come from Him. He has let the earth populate to a grand total that only He knows how many people and who they are. The same way He knows and has named all the stars in heaven.

Therefore you have to think beyond what you see on the earth, and know that God wants us all to operate in the super natural.

That comes with Faith.

Bible Study # 81
From the teachings of Pastor Bill Winston,
Input also by Anita Cameron,
Bible: King James Version (KJV)
4/8/08

"Understanding Our Divinity"

We should imitate our Father. God wants us to act like Him.

You have received righteousness by faith.

We have received everything by the blood of Jesus: Peace, love, hope, joy and righteousness.

The enemy Satan can distort you by making you think what is actually bad, something good, and what's actually good, something bad.

The Holy Spirit is in you to guide you.

You are a spirit with a soul living in a body.

Sin conscientiousness destroys Faith.

Satan tries to destroy your faith by continuing bring up your past, making you feel that your are not right, and because of your past you don't stand a chance of becoming a child of God.

We are complete. We are the righteousness of God.

If you are awake to righteousness, you will not sin.

Faith is a force. God wants condemnation out of your spirit and heart.

He does not want you to feel condemned.

Condemnation will destroy your spirit.

Spiritual Guidance from the Teachings of God's Anointed

In God's eyes you are complete. The blood of Jesus completes you.

When you do something wrong and ask for forgiveness, God does not beat you.

Our divinity is that we are starting from the inside and moving to the outside.

Condemned people don't want others to be free.

There are people who want you to be a slave to something.

We are free, and we will not carry bondage because our Lord and Savior freed us from bondage.

Roman 10: 1
Apostle Paul is writing to other apostles, saying, "Brethren, my heart's desire and prayer to God for Israel is, that they might be saved.

Roman 10: 2
For I bear them record that they have zeal of God, but not according to knowledge.

Roman 10: 3
For they being ignorant of God's righteousness, and going about to establish there own righteousness have not submitted themselves unto the righteousness of God.

The moment you are free and people see it, they start trying to bring up things to you about your past.

The Devil, Satan, is always trying to remind you of what you did.

Don't rehearse it let it go. We are a part of Jesus.

2nd Corinthians 1: 22
Who has also sealed us, and given the earnest of the Spirit in our hearts.

Satan is constantly trying to defeat you. Sickness and disease have no right to live on or in your body, for everything that comes on your body dies.

If God is in you, it can't touch you.

If you walk in the spirit, you have dominion over this world.

Satan is after your dignity. He's trying to make you feel ashamed.

From now on you are crown with honor and glory. Glory is the anointing.

The greatest bondage you can have is a guilty past in your mind.

Don't do that to yourself.

Stop limiting your life with limits.

It is time you understand that you are born again, and that means you are a new creature, born with the blood of Jesus.

Faith is the establishment of righteousness, and the Almighty God in His image created us.

Bible Study # 82
From the teaching of Dr. Charles Stanley,
Input also by Anita Cameron,
Bible: King James Version (KJV)

"When Your Fire Goes Out"

Since being a Christian are you still excited about Jesus Christ, or has the flame died down.

If you have lost interest the fire in your soul cease to be a flame.

The last letter apostle Paul wrote while in a Roman dungeon was to Timothy. Two years later, the Roman Government beheaded Paul.

Paul wrote the letter to Timothy because he was his mentor, and sense something in Timothy that he had become fearful, perhaps losing his faith, or trying to get alone with others and their beliefs and feeling ashamed.

2nd Timothy 1: 5
Paul writes, "When I call to remembrance the unfeigned faith that is in you. Which dwelt fast your grandmother Lois, and your mother Eunice; and I am persuaded that in you also.

*2nd **Timothy 1: 6***
Wherefore I put you in remembrance that you stir up the gift of God, which is in you by the putting on of my hands.

2nd Timothy 1: 7
For God has not given us the spirit of fear, but of power, and of love, and of a sound mind.

2nd Timothy 1: 8
Therefore, don't be ashamed of the testimony of our Lord, nor of me his prisoner: but be you a partaker of the afflictions of the gospel according to the power of God.

2nd Timothy 1: 9
Who has saved us, and called us with a Holy calling, not according to our works, but according to His own purpose and grace, which was given to us in Christ Jesus before the world began.

2nd Timothy 1: 10
But is not made manifest by the appearing of our Savior Jesus Christ, who has abolished death, and has brought life and immortality to light through the gospel.

2nd Timothy 1: 11
Where unto I am appointed a preacher, and an apostle, and a teacher of the Gentiles.

God intended for the flame to be in our life now and forever. Our flame should not flow lowly.

Be cautious, because the flame of your devotion to Christ can die out.

1st Timothy 4: 12
Let no man despise your youth; but be you an example of the believers, in word, in conversation, in charity, in spirit, in faith and impurity.

1st Timothy 1: 3
Paul's writing to Timothy warnings against false teaching, "When I left for Macedonia, I urged you to stay there in Ephesus and stop those who are teaching wrong doctrine.

1st Timothy 1: 4
Don't let people waste time in endless speculation over myths and spiritual pedigrees. For these things only cause arguments, they don't help people live a life of faith in God.

1st Timothy 1: 5
The purpose of my instruction is that all the Christians there would be filled with love that comes from a pure heart, a clear conscience and sincere faith.

1st Timothy 1: 6
But some teachers have missed this whole point. They have turned away from these things and spend their time arguing and talking foolishness.

1st Timothy 1: 7
They want to be known as teachers of the Law of Moses, but they don't know what they are talking about even though they seem so confident.

You don't cool off about God and Christ.

If Satan can get you to forget about God and look to other things, which is a gradual decision made by you through Satan, he will have defeated you and your flame will die down in flowing amber.

How do people detect that this is happening in their life.

1. They began to neglect the Word of God.

   What wood is to a fire, the Word of God is to your life. You can't turn away from the Word.

2. Their prayer life changes.
3. Their church attendance changes.
4. They give occasionally.
5. They began to compromise their beliefs.
6. They become very defensive of their life style.
7. Their sense of security is lost.
8. They began to doubt:
   a. The Power of God.
   b. That God loves them.
   c. The sense of assurance.
9. They cease to listen to the continuing prompting of The Holy Spirit.

   The Holy Spirit's business is to prompt us in our life; to tell us what we are doing right or wrong.

How do you rekindle your fire?

1. Recognize what is happening in your heart.
2. Recall your life when you were a fire for God.
3. Repent of the things that are not right in your life.
4. Refocus your attention to God.

   God did not make our bodies to have tension and anxiety.

5. Read the Word of God daily.

    When you read ask God to speak to your heart.

    The fire will go out if you don't put wood on the fire, that's what happens when you don't keep the flame going in your Christian life.

    Seek the Face of God daily.

    Pray—Lord I am seeking you,
    I want to hear from you, and
    I want an intimate relationship with you.

    Selfishness is not of God.

6. Perseverance.

    Be absorbed in it.

7. Rely upon the Holy Spirit to enable you to understand God's message to us.

    Has the fire in your life dwindled down to ashes or is it still flaming?

Bible Study # 83
Bible study by Anita Cameron
Bible: King James Version and the
New Beginners Bible

"The Power Of The Blood"

The blood has a voice.

The blood of Jesus has more power than we can imagine or comprehend.

Do you know that the blood talks?

Genesis 4:8
And Cain talked with Abel his brother, and it came to pass, when they were in the field, that Cain rose up against his brother, and killed him.

Genesis 4: 9
And The Lord said unto Cain, "Where is Abel your brother?" and he said I know not: Am I my brother's keeper?

Genesis 4: 10
And the Lord said, "What have you done? The voice of your brother's blood cried unto me from the ground.

Abel's blood talked.

Your blood has a connection with our Father and Jesus. Your blood talks to them.

The power of God is so great we cannot imagine.

All souls are mine said the Lord.
I know you inside and out.
I know when you're coming in and going out.
I know what's coming to you in advance: Including temptation.

My Spirit warns your spirit.

The blood Jesus shed for our sins talked.

Every drop He shed talked.

That's why before Jesus became the ultimate sacrifice; the blood of animals took away the sins of the people for a year.

Pharaoh of Egypt would not let the Israelites go. Therefore,

Exodus 11: 4
And Moses said, "Thus said the Lord about midnight will I go out into the midst of Egypt.

Exodus 11: 5
And all the firstborn in the land of Egypt shall die, from the firstborn of Pharaoh, even unto the first born of the maid servant that is behind the mill, and all first born of beasts.

Exodus 12: 1
And the Lord spoke unto Moses and Aaron in the land of Egypt saying,

Exodus 12: 2
This month shall be unto you the beginning of months: It shall be the first month of the year to you.

Exodus 12: 3
Speak unto all the congregation of Israel saying, in the tenth day of this month they shall take to them every man a lamb, according to the house of their fathers; a lamb for a house.

Exodus 12: 5
Your lamb should be without blemish, a male of the first year: you shall take it out from the sheep, or from the goats.

Exodus 12: 6
And you shall keep it up until the fourteenth of the same month: and the whole assembly of the congregation of Israel shall kill it in the evening.

Exodus 12: 7
And they shall take of the blood and strike it on the two side's posts and on the upper doorpost of the houses, wherein they shall eat it.

Exodus 12: 13
And the blood shall be to you for a token upon the houses where you are: and when I see the blood, I will pass over you, and the plague shall not be upon you to destroy you, when I smite the land of Egypt.

That's why the Blood of Jesus' is the ultimate sacrifice. His blood covers the believers to eternity.

Now those people that are not under the blood of Jesus, when death comes they die.

But those of us that are under the blood of Jesus, death will past us by and our spirit and soul goes up to heaven at our last breath on this earth for eternity.

When a person sheds another person's blood it is not a secret, God and Jesus knows, because the blood calls out to them.

The blood in your body is sacred you cannot live with out it.

From the moment you are born and separated from your mother's wound blood comes into your body from God. That blood gives you life.

In order for us to live blood circulates throughout our body day and night. The moment it stops the body is dead. But we the believers our spirit and soul go straight to heaven at the last breath on earth.

NBB Romans 5:9
And since we have been made right in God's sight by the blood of Christ, He will certainly save us from God's judgment.

KJV Romans 5: 9
Much more then, being now justified by His blood, we shall be saved from wrath through Him.

1ˢᵗ Corinthians 11: 25
In the way, Jesus took the cup of wine after supper saying, "This cup is the new covenant between God and you, sealed by the shedding of my blood.

Ephesians 1: 7
In whom we have redemption through His blood, the forgiveness of sins, according to the riches of His grace.

Hebrew 9: 22
And almost all things are by the law purged with blood; and without shedding of blood is no remission.

NBB Hebrew 9: 22
In fact we can say that according to the Law of Moses, nearly everything was purified by the sprinkling with blood. Without the shedding of blood, there is no forgiveness of sins.

1ˢᵗ Peter 1: 19
He paid for us with the precious lifeblood of Christ, the sinless, spotless Lamb of God.

Bible Study # 84
From the teachings of Dr. Charles Stanley,
Input also by Anita Cameron.
Bible: Kings James Version (KJV)
New Beginners Bible (NBB)

"Protecting Your Future"

A mistake people often make is sacrificing their future for the pleasure of the present moment.

In Genesis 25: 27-30
Tells about how Esau, the oldest son of Isaac sold his birthright to his brother Jacob for a bowl of soup. He came in hungry and gave away his birthright, which was of a significant value in those days. The first born was the most valued and blessed by God through his father Isaac. The bible states that Esau despised his birthright.

1. When you are blind to the values in life, your future makes another turn.

   How many people do you know have sacrificed there future for the pleasure of the present moment?

   Let's look at:

   a. A drug addict.
   b. A person in jail.
   c. A person with an attitude.
   d. A thief.
   e. A Murderer.
   f. A person's pride took over their soul.
   g. A person having extra marital relations.
   h. A person putting material things before God.
   i. A person who feels going to school is a waste of time and stop going.

2. When you are blind to the value of life you take another path.

   That path can impact your whole life. Your business, money, prestige, recognition, and family can be neglected. Then you will find yourself without your family and all the things that you have worked for.

   When you are ruled by your appetite rather than the Spirit of God, your path and your future takes another turn.

   Everyday we are responsible for controlling our emotions.

When people are ruled by their appetite, it's always what they want, what they see, what they feel and what they touch. It pours in their minds.

   And example of this is look at our job market and our home situation.

   We that are believers will be sent a warning telling us, don't do that, don't marry that person, don't go that way, and don't take that job.

   Satan tells you why not! There it is, you want it, take it.

   You take something that is not of God, you will pay for it.

   When you refuse to speak and respond to the Spirit of God you are backing off. You must live by the wisdom of God.

3. When you require immediate gratification, meaning I want it now, you are saying you're smarter than God, and sometimes we are not ready for what we want.

   Then we say if only I knew what was going to happen, I would not have done that, but remember you were warned.

   How many people have married the wrong person? If we are willing to wait, He will join us to the right person.

   How many people have said, "I have forfeited what I could have had? I have sacrificed my future because I wasn't willing to wait for the best. Most of us have.

Do you think you are going to get God's best by doing it your way by having it now?

Many people fall prey to money on the table and sex, without thinking of the consequences.

Ask yourself, "Do I want what I want now or do I want what God has for me?"

4. When you focus on temporal moments instead of Spiritual Heritage and an eternal future, your future is a gamble.

You must think before you make a decision. Think to yourself is this a temporal or an eternal decision?

Nothing will be in the casket with that body.

We came in this world naked, and when we leave spirit and soul goes up, and that body is empty.

Always remember,
When Satan is most dangerous to you is when you are:

a. Hungry
b. Angry
c. Lonely
d. Tired

Satan begins to feed your mind with things like,

1. Why don't you go to the mall?
2. Find someone to spend the night with.

What is the bowl of soup in your life?

Do you risk peace, joy happiness and a feeling of tranquillity?

Remember we reap what we sow, be it now or in the future.

5. When you have no respect for Spiritual things.

    You have no respect for the Word of God, especially when you say. "Don't tell me about church or about the Word of God.

    The Bible is God's instruction for us in life. How we are to live.

6. When you fail to consider the future consequence.

    Don't make foolish decision that will cost you for the rest of your life.

    Is there anything in your life worth going to hell for?

In the bible God wanted to use Samson for His purpose, but Samson allowed pride, lust and self-confidence to ruin his potential. He gave up his secret of strength to a woman named Delilah who tricked him, and called in a man to shave off his hair, because that's where his strength came from.

Judges 16: 21
So the Philistines captured him and gouged out his eyes. They took him to Gaza, where he was bound with bronze chains and made to grind grain in the prison.

The bible also states how King David sins with Bathsheba. David underestimates his potential to fall when he allows lust to control his thoughts. He soon discovers that one act of passion can lead to a lifetime of regret.

You can read the story in the book of Samuel Chapter 11

David saw Bathsheba, a married woman taking a bath as he looked out of his window, and had lust for her. He being the King called for her and got her pregnant. Then King David arranged for Uriah's Bathsheba's husband's death, by having him placed at the front line doing the war.

The law is what you sow, you shall reap.

If you are wise, you will receive Jesus in your life.

There is nothing worth dying for without Jesus in your life.

Bible Study # 85
From the teachings of Dr. Charles Stanley,
Input also by Anita Cameron,
Bible: King James Version (KJV)

"Our God Of Grace"

Grace is God's riches at Christ's expense.

Christian life is living under Grace.

God hates pride.

Pastor Doug Batchelar states, "The more spiritually proud you become the more spiritually poor you are. But those who recognize and admit their sorry spiritual state in life, who knows they can be saved only by the Grace of Christ, have an advantage in their humility." Jesus promises them, "Blessed are the poor in spirit for theirs is the kingdom of heaven.

Jesus paid our sin debt in full and that's God's gift to us.

Hebrew 4: 14
Seeing then that we have a great high priest that is passed into the heavens, Jesus the Son of God, let us hold fast our profession.

Hebrew 4: 15
For we have not an high priest which cannot be touched with the feeling in our infirmities; but was in all points tempted like as we are, yet without sin.

Hebrew 4: 16
Let us therefore come boldly unto the throne of grace that we may obtain mercy, and find grace to help in time of need.

Those who have never trusted Jesus Christ as their Savior do not adhere to His Grace.

"The Throne of Grace"

Revelation 20: 11
And I saw a great white throne, and Him that sat on it, from whose face the earth and the heaven fled away; and there was found no place for them.

Revelation 20: 12
I saw the dead, small and great, stand before God; and the books were opened: and another book was opened, which is the book of life: and the dead were judged out of those things which were written in the books, according to their works.

Revelation 20: 13
And the sea gave up the dead which were in it; and death and hell delivered up the dead which were in them: and they were judged every man according to their works.

Revelation 20: 14
And the death and hell were cast into the lake of fire. This is the second death.

Revelation 20: 15
And whosoever was not found written in the book of life was cast into the lake of fire.

There's a place we can go when we have needs, and when we are hurt, that includes everything we need and desire of His will not what we earn but under His Grace.

As believers we should be the humble ones because it's the pure Grace of God.

Your entire life is lived by the Grace of God.

His goodness, mercy, loving and kindness surround you.

Mercy—God does not give us what we deserve, because we are all sinners.

Our human mind cannot imagine a sinless person like Jesus, because He took away our sins and went to the right hand of the Father.

Grace—God give us what we don't deserve.

We live in grace everyday.

How God expresses His grace to us.

Ephesians 1: 3
Blessed be the God and Father of our Lord Jesus Christ, who has blessed us all with spiritual blessings in heavenly places in Christ. (Gifts)

Ephesians 1: 4
According as He has chosen us in Him before the foundation of the world, that we should be holy and without blame before Him in love.

Ephesians 1: 5
He has chosen and predestined us. He put a circle around us, and said they are my children.

"The Heart of Grace"

Romans 3:23
For all have sinned, and come short of the glory of God.

Romans 3: 24
Being justified freely by His grace through the redemption that is in Christ Jesus.

Romans 3: 25
Who God has set forth to be propitiation through faith in His blood, to declare His righteousness for the remission of sins that are past, through the forbearance of God.

Romans 3: 26
To declare, I say, at this time His righteousness: That He might be just and justifier of Him, which believe in Jesus.

When God created us He expected us to live and be fruitful and multiply living freely in the Garden of Eden. But, because of Adam's sin, God said everyone would die.

God saw the helplessness of man therefore He sent His only Son as a substitute for our life.

It was God who killed His Son for us. Jesus is the ultimate sacrifice.

We have been forgiven of our sins, if we accept Jesus as our Lord and Savior and walk in His way.

By His Grace we have gained an eternal position in heaven.

Ephesians 2: 1
And you have He quicken, who were dead in trespasses and sins.

Ephesians 2: 2
Where in time past walked according to the course of this world, according to the prince of the power of the air, the spirit that now worked in the children of disobedience.

*Ephesians **2: 3***
Among whom also we all had our conversation in times past in the lusts of our flesh, fulfilling the desires of the flesh and of the mind; and were by nature the children of wrath, even as others.

Ephesians 2: 4
But God who is rich in mercy, for His great love wherewith He loved us.

Ephesians 2:5
Even when we were dead in sins, have quickened us together with Christ (by grace you are saved).

Ephesians 2: 6
And has raised us up together; and made us sit together in heavenly places in Christ Jesus.

Ephesians 2: 7
That in the ages to come He might show the exceeding riches of His grace in His kindness toward us through Christ Jesus.

Ephesians 2: 8
For by grace are you saved through faith; and that not of yourselves: It is the gift of God.

You are a trophy to the Grace of God.

By His Grace we can endure suffering and profit from it.

2nd Corinthians 12: 8
Paul said, "For this thing I besought the Lord three times, that it might depart from me."

2nd Corinthians 12: 9
And the Lord said unto me. My grace is sufficient for you: For my strength is made perfect in weakness. Most gladly Paul said, therefore will I rather glory in my infirmities that the power of Christ may rest upon me.

In our difficulties it is the Grace of God that makes us adequate and sufficient.

*1st **Peter 5: 10***
But the God of all Grace, who has called us unto His eternal glory by Christ Jesus, after that you have suffered a while, make you perfect, establish, strengthened, settle you.

1st Peter 5: 11
To Him be glory and dominion forever and ever, A Men.

By His Grace He has called us to serve Him.

Galatians 1: 1
Paul, an Apostle (not of men, neither by man, but by Jesus Christ, and God the Father, who raised Him from the dead).

*Galatians **1: 2***
And all the brothers which are with me. Unto the churches of Galatia,

Galatians 1: 3
Grace be to you and peace from God the Father, and from our Lord Jesus Christ.

Galatians 1: 4
Who gave Himself for our sins, that He might deliver us from the present evil world, according to the will of God and our Father.

NBB—Galatians 1: 5
That is why glory belongs to God through all the ages of eternity. Amen

NBB—Galatians 1: 6
I am shocked that you are turning away so soon from God, who in His love and mercy called you to share the eternal life He gives through Christ. You are already following a different way.

Galatians 1: 15
But when it pleased God, who separated me from my mother's womb, and called me by His Grace.

Galatians 1: 16
To reveal His Son in me, that I might preach Him among the heathens, immediately I conferred not with flesh and blood.

God called Paul to minister and we are all called to serve God.

By His Grace He has equipped us with spiritual gifts.

Romans 12: 6
Having then gifts differing according to the grace that is given us, whether prophecy, let us prophesy according to the proportion of faith.

Romans 12: 7
Or ministry let us wait on our ministering or he that teaches, on teaching.

Romans 12: 8
Or he that exhort, on exhortation: he that gives, let Him do it with simplicity; he that rule, with diligence; he that show mercy, with cheerfulness.

He will never call us to do more that we can bare.

By His Grace He provides everything we need.

2nd Corinthians 9: 6
But this I say, he which sow sparingly shall reap sparingly; and he, which sow bountifully, shall reap also bountifully.

2nd Corinthians 9: 7
Every man according as he purposed in his heart, so let him give; not grudgingly, or necessity: for God loves a cheerful giver.

2nd Corinthians 9: 8
And God is able to make all grace abound towards you; that you, always having all sufficiency in all things, may abound to every good work.

Before the foundation of the earth He chose you by grace.

We can never boast about anything. Everything we have achieved is by the grace of God.

When we reject our Lord and Savior Jesus Christ, we are rejecting our greatest gift given to us by God.

To die without Christ, a person will have to stand before God and say they have rejected His greatest gift, His Son Jesus our Lord and Savior.

We have to receive it, believe it and take it to ourselves.

Pray—God open my eyes and let me see something for me.

Bible Study # 86
July 4, 2008
Bible study by Anita Cameron
Bible: King James Version and the
New Beginners Bible.

"Hell Is Real"

We often hear about hell on earth. Usually our hell on earth stems from the decisions we have made.

We also hear about the hell of damnation after death, which also stems from the decisions we have made doing our lifetime.

That's why it is so important to have Jesus in your life, so that when temptations come, the Holy Spirit will warn you and if you take heed to what He's saying, you will be guided into another direction.

But quite often we don't want to hear or listen to our warnings. We want what we feel and turn away from the warnings.

Our final evaluations always consist of: What Happened?

a. How did I get into this and how can I get out?
b. Why is this happening to me?
c. What did I do to deserve this?
d. Then we call on the Lord for help.

All we had to do was to pray to the Lord for guidance before hand.

Its takes a while to know a good thing, and it takes a while to know a bad thing. One thing for sure we should not rush into anything. We should always first pray to the Lord for guidance.

Hell on earth is quite different from the hell of damnation.

The hell on earth can be corrected. But the hell of damnation cannot.

Many people don't believe in the hell of damnation, but I can assure you its true because the Word of God says it true.

In the book of Luke chapters 16: 19-31 is a story about hell.

Luke 16: 19
Jesus said, "There was a certain rich man, which was clothed in purple and fine linen, and fared sumptuously everyday.

Luke 16:20
And there was a certain beggar named Lazarus, which was laid at his gate full of sores.

Luke 16: 21
And desiring to be fed with the crumbs which fell from the rich man's table; moreover the dogs came and licked his sores.

This is and example of a person with money looking down on other people that are not as fortunate as they are, and also having no concern about them.

Luke 16: 22
And it came to pass that the beggar died, and was carried by the angels into Abraham's bosom: The rich man also died, and was buried.

Luke 16: 23
And in hell he the rich man lifted up his eyes, being in torments, and see Abraham afar off, and Lazarus in his bosom.

Luke 16: 24
And he cried and said, father Abraham, have mercy on me, and send Lazarus, that he may dip the tip of his finger in water, and cool my tongue: For I am tormented in this flame.

Luke 16: 25
But Abraham said son, remember that in your lifetime you received good things, and like wise Lazarus evil things: But now he is comforted, and you are tormented.

Luke 16: 26
And beside all this, between us and you there is a great gulf fixed: So that they which pass from here to you cannot: Neither can they pass to us that would come from there.

Meaning once you are in hell you cannot get help from anyone in heaven, and you cannot get out, because God has placed something there forbidding it.

Like 16: 27
Then he said I pray thee therefore father that you would send him to my father's house.

Luke 16: 28
For I have five brothers, that he may testify unto them, unless they also come into thiis place of torment.

Luke 16: 29
Abraham said unto him, they have Moses and the prophets; let them hear them.

Luke 16: 30
And he said, no, father Abraham; but if one went unto them from the dead, they will repent.

Luke 16: 31
And Abraham said unto him, if they hear not Moses and the prophets, neither will they be persuaded, if one rose from the dead."

Meaning, there are people on earth, know matter what they see or told, they are full of unbelief.
You have to choose between evil and good.

Luke 16:12
No servant can serve two masters, for either he will hate the one, and love the other, or else he will hold to the one, and despise the other. You cannot serve God and Mammon.

You cannot love the Lord and serve that devil Satan. When you believe that Jesus is your Lord and savior, who suffered and died to save you, and receive Him in your heart, you are heaven bound. If you decide to choose the other direction you are hell bound.

2nd Peter 2: 4
For if God spared not the angels that sinned, but delivered them down to hell, and delivered them into chains of darkness, to be reserved unto judgment.

The same can happen to you if you don't repent.

2nd Peter 2: 9
The Lord knows how to deliver the godly out of temptations, and to reserve the unjust unto the Day of Judgment to be punished.

Bible Study # 87
From the teaching of Pastor Anthony L. Hines,
From Winston Salem, NC
Input also by Anita Cameron,
Bible: King James Version,
New Beginners Bible

"The Truth Is Salvation"

John 10: 11
Jesus said, "I am the good Shepherd: The good Shepherd gave His life for the sheep (meaning us).

Romans 10: 9
If you shall confess with your mouth the Lord Jesus, and shall believe in your heart that God has raised Him from the dead, you will be saved.

Romans 10: 10
For it is by believing in your heart that you are made right with God, and it is by confessing with your mouth that you are saved.

Romans 10: 11
For the scripture said, whosoever Believe in Him Shall Not Be Ashamed.

Romans 10: 12
For there is no difference between the Jew and the Greek (Gentile): For the same Lord over all is rich unto all that call upon Him.

Romans 10: 13
FOR WHOSOEVER SHALL CALL THE NAME OF THE LORD SHALL BE SAVED.

SALVATION comes from trusting Christ.
And when you do you will receive the following:

a. Peace
b. Healing

c. Protection
d. Deliverance
e. You're Preserved
f. You're Rescued
g. Strengthen
h. Recovery from fatality

Salvation involves all of these and more.

Many Christians have not received all of the above because they don't believe they can receive, their faith is minimum.

Satan will always sale us lies. When we fall for them and mess up our life, he walks away laughing and goes straight to the Lord to make a report on us.

John 10: 10
Jesus said, "The thief (Satan) comes not, but to steal, and to kill and to destroy: Jesus said, "I am come that they might have life and that they might have it abundantly.

The Lord Jesus will never leave you. He is our Good Shepherd.

Psalm 46: 1
God is our refuge and strength, a very present help in trouble.

Satan's job is to keep us at a place of procrastination, so that we aren't doing anything.

3rd John 1: 2
Beloved I wish above all things that you may prosper and be in health as your soul prospers.

God's desire is for us to prosper and have no stress or worries.

But when we are unwilling to pursue change by not doing for instance, reading more to enhance our life, work on our attitudes, calm ourselves down and accept constructive criticism, then our mind, will and soul will not be on the same page, causing trouble and confusion in our life.

Some people will bring up other people's past in order to justify what they are doing. Instead of trying to cover up what they are doing they should learn from other's experiences. When someone tells you about their past to help you, listen and learn.

Even though the Lord puts in our spirit; don't you remember what happened before when you did that?

Yet we don't listen. It's always about I and me, and what I want.

There are many people blessed with a job yet they want to do half the work. When they are told how much time they are allowed to take for a break, and lunch, they decide to take additional time.

They spend a lot of valuable time planning on how they can keep from doing their job.

When you over extend you are over extended.

Remember what you reap you shall sow

God cannot give you a new house, car etc., and you don't take care of what you already have.

Many Christians wonder why they don't have certain things and why are they struggling.

They feel that God is going to do everything and they don't have to do nothing.

The truth is you must step out on faith, trust in the Lord and stop procrastinating.

You cannot sit home and do nothing about your dreams.

Remember Satan wants you to procrastinate so as time go by you will become more like he wants you to become. Satan wants you to be stressed, depressed, feeling insecure to the point where you will look for pills, and other drugs to validate you.

For our salvation all we need is the Lord because His Angels are there to protect us, and The Holy Spirit is there to guide us.

The Lord can't bless some of us because we won't let Him. Yet He loves us and will never leave us.

Bible Study # 88
From the teaching of Dr. Charles Stanley
Input also Anita Cameron
Bible: King James Version and
New Beginners Bible

"Dealing With False Teaching"

Matthew 24: 11
Jesus said, "Many false prophets shall rise and deceive many.

Matthew 24:24
For there shall arise false Christ, and false prophets, and shall show great signs and wonders, in so much that, if it were possible, they shall deceive the very elect.

There are many false teachers in the world and most are charismatic, having a gift of gab (talking).

You will find many false teachers in all religions.

1. False teachers build cults in order to have ultimate control over people.
2. False teachers are deceivers.
3. False teachers will brainwash people into believing that, they are the Messiah and that God told them so.

Mark 13: 5
Jesus said, "Take heed lest any man deceive you.

Mark 13: 6
For many shall come in my name saying, I am Christ: and shall deceive many.

4. False teachers will indoctrinate; they want people to believe in what they say. When they do bring up the bible they reword the bible in order to elevate themselves.
5. False teachers demand obedience. They tell the people what they can and cannot do or else.

6. False teachers Isolate people from family and friends in order to keep control.
7. False teachers use psychological conditions; children become victims, usually it involves sex.
8. False teachers use deception; they lead people to do wrong.

> False teachers in the churches say they don't believe everything in the bible, thereby dividing the churches.

> Some weave their own unbelief in church, and some confess their own belief in the word of God.

> Some relate a universal belief that everyone is going to get to heaven. That is an untruth. We are all not going to get to heaven.

9. False teachers are destructive: They don't want to talk about the Holy Spirit.

> *Galatians 3: 1*
> *Paul says to the Galatians, "Oh, foolish Galatians! What magician has cast an evil spell on you? For you used to see the meaning of Jesus Christ's death as clearly as though I had shown you a signboard with a picture of Christ dying on the cross.*

> *Galatians 3: 2*
> *Let me ask you this one question: Did you receive the Holy Spirit by keeping the law? Of course not, for the Holy Spirit came upon you only after you believed the message you heard about Christ.*

> God's Word is Authority

10. False teachers usually start their own church. They find people that are needy and don't know much about the bible.

> The foundation of the truth is the bible.

> False teachers are not up to bringing you up to the word of God.

> *Dangers of following a false teacher:*

   a. You will be deceived.
   b. You will be divided from church and family.
   c. You will be disillusioned.

When a person departs from the word of God, they will feel a sense of emptiness.
There is danger departing from God's word.

1st Timothy 4: 1
Now the Spirit speak expressly that in latter times some shall depart from the faith, giving heed to seducing spirits, and doctrines of devils.

False teaching can destroy people.

How can we protect ourselves from being fooled?

1. Cling to the word of God as your faithful guidance.
2. Study the word of God under a trustworthy teacher.

    A trustworthy teacher does not question the word of God and the truth of it. His teaching keeps in the word of God.

3. Learn to refute false doctrine: You refute it by saying I read it in the word of God the bible.

People will tell you something they feel you want to hear and not convict you of your sins, thereby keeping you from converting from your sins.

Many false teachers are saying Jesus is not coming back, because He came back already. They are wrong.

Matthew 24: 23
Jesus said, "If any man shall say unto you look, here is Christ, or there: Believe it not."

Matthew 24: 26
Jesus said, "Wherefore if they shall say unto you, behold, He is in the desert; go not forth, behold, He is in the secret chamber: believe it not."

Jesus is coming back.

Matthew 24: 29
Jesus said, "Immediately after the tribulations of those days shall the sun be darkened, and the moon shall not give her light, and the stars shall fall from heaven, and the powers of the heaven shall be shaken.

Matthew 24: 30
And then shall appear the sign of the Son of man in heaven: and then shall all the tribes of the earth mourn, and they shall see the Son of man coming in the clouds of heaven with power and great glory.

Matthew 24: 31
And He shall send His Angles with a great sound of a trumpet, and they shall gather together His elect from the four winds, from one end of heaven to the other.

Read the word and be on guard against false doctrine.

2nd John 7
For many deceivers are entered into the world who confess not that Jesus Christ is come in the flesh. This is a deceiver and an anti-Christ.

2nd John 8
Look to yourselves, that we lose not those things which we have wrought, but that we receive a full reward.

2nd John 9
Whosoever transgressed, and abides not in the doctrine of Christ, have not God. He that abide in the doctrine of Christ he has both the Father and the Son.

2nd John 10
If there come any unto you, and bring not this doctrine receive him/her not into your house, neither bid him/her God's speed.

People will come to your house to mislead you.

How do they come?

1. To your door.
2. Through the television.
3. Through E-Mails.
4. By telephone.
5. By Mail.

You have no obligation to let anyone or anything in your house that will deceive you.

Read the bible for your own knowledge, wisdom and understanding and the
Holy Spirit will help you.

Bible Study # 89
From the teaching of Dr. Charles Stanley,
Input also by Anita Cameron
Bible: King James Version and
New Beginners Bible

"Can God Use you?"

It is the will of God that we serve Him.

God has planned to use everyone.

When we do good works we are serving Him.

I am not talking about being in church only. It is what you are doing at work, home, in your community to enable others.

He created us as human beans to serve Him.

He uses children also.

No Christian has the right to waste their life.

You are either going to obey God or the devil.

Jesus purchased us in full with His blood so that we could be accepted in God's eyes and enabled us to live with Him.

The body of Christ should be energetic people filled with energy and spirit.

God has provided what we need so that He can use us.

He's given us certain talents to enable each other.

Our talent is to be used to enable others.

Suppose there were no automobile mechanics. How would our cars get fixed of serviced.

Suppose there were no talents given to people that would be able to make street lights, railroads, planes, trains, purify water and many other things we take for granted.

Suppose there were no nurses, doctors or medical facilities.

Whatever skill He gives us it is suppose to impact the people around us.

Each one of us is given gifts.

1st Peter 4: 9
Use hospitality one to another without grudging.

1st Peter 4: 10
As every man has received the gift, even so minister the same one to another, as good stewards of the manifold grace of God.

The gifts that He gives us help people.

Every single one of us is responsible to God for gifts He gives us.

1st Peter 4: 11
If any man speak let him speak as the oracles of God; if any man minister, let him do it as of the ability which God give. That God in all things may be glorified through Jesus Christ, to whom be praise and dominion forever and ever. Amen.

We are to share ourselves for the good. We do it by the strength God provides us with.

He will never ask you to do something you cannot do.

Jesus said before He died, "I am going to send you a helper."

The Holy Spirit will be with you on the earth until your last breath.

Once you accept the grace of God, you are sealed with the Spirit and will be able to carry out your work for others.

Those that are self-centered do not believe they receive what they have from God. Most feel by their own power and education they have accomplished what they have. They are wrong.

Many people refuse to be used by God.
Their hindrances to serving God are:

1. They have a poor-self image.
2. They feel unworthy. We all feel that way.
3. They feel inadequate. We all feel that way.

There's not any one of us that feel adequate in serving God.

We grow by following God when He challenges us to do something. But those that wait on the Lord shall renew their strength; they shall mount up as wings of an eagle; they shall run and not be weary; they shall walk and not faint.

4. They are programmed negatively from childhood.—A parent or people told them they cannot do or will never be able to do anything.
5. They have fear—afraid of being criticize.

When you do not use your talents they are taken away from you and given to someone else.

In Matthews 25: 14-28
Jesus tells a story about three men that were given talents. Two of the men doubled their talents, but one man buried his. When they were ask to make a report the two men that doubled theirs were rewarded and the one that didn't do anything with his, his was taken away and given to the one that had the most.

Matthew 25: 29
To those who use well what they are given, even more will be given, and they will have abundance. But from those who are unfaithful, even what little they have will be taken away

God wants us to take the cross of Jesus and tell someone else, and they tell someone else and it will go all over the world.

6. They are selfish and self-centered—It's all about me myself and I and my future and money.

> When you spend time on your knees and spend time with God He will give you time.

> We forget He created us.

> Life began with Jesus.

7. They are sinners.—You will not serve God faithfully and live in sin.

> God uses us to the degree of:

1. Our potential.
2. Our availability. Could you image saying to God I am not available.
3. Our motivation.
4. Our purity.—How we think or act.

> God sometimes take unlikely people; for instance:

    a. He took a bunch of fisherman and got into their hearts and made them fisher of men.
    b. He used Noah who was a drunk.
    c. He used Abraham who was old.
    d. He used Jacob who was liar.
    e. He used Moses who stuttered.
    f. He used Samson who was a womanizer.

> And God used every one of them for the benefit of us.

> All of us have a lot to offer that we cannot imagine.

> God intend for us to serve Him for the rest of our lives.

> If it's in your heart to say, say these words;

Lord I heard your message. I don't know what to do at this point. But today I will serve you. Whatever you call me to do. I need your help; I am going to trust you to help me. I am making myself available.

Bible Study # 90
From the teaching of Pastor Bill Winston,
Input also by Anita Cameron and
Bishop Noel Jones
Bible: King James Version

"Revelation of Royalty"

Once you believe in God and have faith you become part of His kingdom and you are royalty. We are a kingdom of people.

Jesus is King of kings and Lord of lords.

Revelations 19: 16
And He has on His vesture and on His thigh a name written, KING OF Kings AND LORD OF LORDS.

Psalm 115: 16
The heavens, even the heavens are the Lord's; But the earth has He given to the children of men.

The Spirit inside of God and Jesus is inside of you. You are a child of God. We are to take charge and take back. We are kingdom minded people.

Mark 4: 37
And there arose a great storm of wind, and the waves beat into the ship, so that it was now full.

Mark 4: 38
Jesus was in the hinder part of the ship, asleep on a pillow: and they awake Him, and said unto Him. Master, care thou not that we perish?

Mark 4: 39
And He arose and rebuked the wind, and said unto the sea, peace, be still, and the wind ceased and there was a great calm.

Mark 4: 40
And He said unto them, "Why are you so fearful? How is it that you have no faith?"

Mark 5: 1
And they came over unto the other side of the sea into the country of the Gadarenes:

Mark 5: 2
And when He came out of the ship, immediately there met Him out of the tombs a man with an unclean spirit.

Mark: 5: 3
Who had his dwelling among the tombs; (graves) and no man could bind him, not with chains:

Mark 5: 4
Because he had been often bound with fetters and chains, and the chains had been plucked asunder by him, and the fetters broken in pieces: neither could any man tame him.

Mark 5: 5
And always night and day, he was in the mountains, and in the tombs, crying and cutting himself with stone.

Mark 5: 6
But when he saw Jesus afar off, he ran and worshipped Him.

Mark 5: 7
And he cried with a loud voice, and said, "What have I to do with thee, Jesus, thou Son of the most high God?" I adjure thee by God, that you torment me not.

Mark 5: 8
Jesus said unto him, come out of the man, you unclean spirit.

Mark 5: 9
And Jesus asked him, "What is your name? and he answered, saying my name is legion: for we are many.

The demon legion was the leader and strongman that was holding the whole coast line.

It shows that even all demons recognizes the power of Jesus.

It's a shame that all people do not recognize that we have been given through the blood of Jesus power over Satan and his demons. We have the power to rebuke them in the name of Jesus.

Jesus took back from Satan what was lost when Adam and Eve sinned, and gave it back to God's children on earth, meaning us the children of God given to Jesus by God.

The devil Satan gives people a distorted picture of what God is about.

God loves us so much, that He gave His only begotten Son as an ultimate sacrifice to save us and to give us everlasting life.

Jesus gave Himself for us.

1st John 4:8
He that loves not, know not God; for God is love.

It time we start taking charge. It's time for the church to take over.

The church is working in darkness.

The church is suppose to release the people from the control of Satan. Instead, the churches are letting the people control the churches that are being controlled by Satan.

Changing the wording in the bible to fit their beliefs, so that they can be in control of the congregation.

Most famous people start off in the church, then when they become wealthy Satan takes over them.

In other words they forget where they started from and through the power of Jesus that's why they are where they are. But many people began to feel that by themselves they have achieved.

We cannot achieve anything without Jesus.

Satan might fool you for awhile that you have done this and that by yourself, and you have the power. But when trials and tribulations comes, that's when you realize who has the power, God has the power.

Seek you first the kingdom of God and all you need will be added to you.

You will be in control of your finance, and your peace of mind. We are going to take charge. We will not let demons take over us.

Jesus came to bring a superior system. You are here to take charge and God wants us to take charge.

Isaiah 51: 15
But I am the Lord thy God, that divided the seas, whose waves roared: The Lord of hosts is His name.

Isaiah 51: 16
And I have put my words in your mouth, and I have covered you in the shadow of mine hand, that I may plant the heavens, and lay the foundations of the earth, and say unto Zion, you are my people.

We are to rest in the provision of the Father.

We are the ambassador to Christ.

What we are talking about is break through.

Break through means we have to obey the law of association. All you have to do is show me your friends and I will show you your future. It might be family or church people, that you might have to get away from.

Your spirit comes from God and when you act outside of the spirit you are moving away from God.

You must proclaim the Spirit of God.

You are sealed by the Holy Spirit in heavenly places. You are a child of God.

Remember Jesus stripped Satan of all he had and took it back and gave it to us.

Bishop Noel Jones says,

"Take your place back. And say, this is my place and my space and I will not let Satan take it from me or run away with it.

God restored the man in the world. Satan is not coming in my mind and making me feel depressed, insecure, taking away my joy. You must first take it back in your spirit and mind.

You don't know where you're going, but you know you are going somewhere.

The name of Jesus, what a name.

God is going to make you laugh.

Say, in the name of Jesus, I bind low self-esteem, depression, every demon spirit, impatience, sickness and disease.

I loose peace, finances, joy, love and out of bondage.

Move in your place.

We are royalty part of God's kingdom.

Message from the heart
By Anita Cameron

There are times when we stay into a situation that's not healthy, but because of our fears and insecurities, and not wanting people to think a certain way about us, we stay.

But our Lord who is omniscience—Knows all things
And is omnipotence—have power over all things
And is omnipresent—always present,
Will take you out of that situation, and place you where you are to be.

Sometimes we don't know what's happening to us, but if you look to the Lord where all our help comes from, you will see He has something better for us.

So be patient and praise the Lord everyday for His goodness and mercy towards you.

Satan is trying to come in and destroy your faith. Recognize Him and say, "I am a child of God. He loves and watches over me. Everything is going to be all right. I have peace and joy eventhough I am going through tough times."

Isaiah 54:17
No weapon that is formed against you shall prosper; and every tongue that shall rise against you in judgment thou shall condemn. This is the heritage of the servants of the Lord, and their righteousness is of me, said the Lord.

Song written by me and words
given to me supernaturally.

"That When I Knew I Was Heaven Bound"

He lifted me up, when I was down,
He lifted me up; I was almost to the ground,
He said to me, "I've set you free."
That's when I knew, I was heaven bound.

He said to me "I've set you free,
I've set you free on Calvery,
He said to me, I've got the key,
Your ticket to heaven is on me."

Chorus

He Lifted me up, when I was down,
He lifted me up; I was almost to the ground,
He said to me, "I've set you free."
That's when I knew, I was heaven bound.

He said to me, "You must believe,
You must have faith and trust in me indeed,
You must keep my words in your heart.
Forever together we will never part.

Chorus

He lifted me up, when I was down.
He lifted me up; I was almost to the ground,
He said to me, "I've set you free."
That's when I knew, I was heaven bound.

He gives me strength, from day to day,
He guides and sends me on my merry way,
He speaks to me, and when I pray,
I know He hears me and is with me everyday.

Chorus

He lifted me up, when I was down,
He lifted me up; I was almost to the ground,
He said to me, "I've set you free."
That's when I knew, I was heaven bound.

Song written by Anita Joy Cameron
given to me supernaturally

"Remember Who Died For You"

Where ever you may go,
Whatever you may do,
Whatever pain you feel
Remember who died for you.

No matter how things seem
No matter what you feel life brings,
No matter what people have done to you,
Remember who died for you.

He took away all our sins, so we can have life eternity.
He was in heaven from the beginning of time, yet
He came down to earth to free you and me.

If you call His name Jesus
He will be right there for you.
Keep in your heart His words are true
and you will have peace know matter
what you're going through.
So keep your heart and mind focus,
And remember who died for you.